GREAT TOASTS

FROM BIRTHS TO WEDDINGS TO RETIREMENT PARTIES...AND
EVERYTHING IN BETWEEN

By
Andrew Frothingham

CASTLE BOOKS

This edition published in 2005 by
CASTLE BOOKS ®
A division of Book Sales, Inc.
114 Northfield Avenue
Edison, NJ 08837

This edition published by arrangement with
Career Press
3 Tice Road
Franklin Lakes, NJ 07417

Great Toasts © 2002 Andrew Frothingham.
Original English language edition published by Career Press

Great Toasts
Edited and Typeset by KATE PRESTON

Library of Congress Cataloging-in-Publication Data

Frothingham, Andrew.
Great toasts : from births to weddings to retirement parties--and everything
in between / by Andrew Frothingham.
p. cm.
        Includes index.
        1.   Toasts. I. Title.

PN6341 .F77 2002   2002022122
808.5'1—dc21

ISBN-13: 978-0-7858-2107-6
ISBN-10: 0-7858-2107-4

Printed in the United States of America

Dedication

Here's to Harry!
If he had lived a bit longer, we'd have written this together.

Contents

Introduction

oasting is a wonderful way to share your feelings with other people. While many people are reluctant to get up and deliver a full-blown speech, almost everyone, with a little preparation and practice, can shine in public while toasting. Toasts are most often shorter than speeches, but they can be every bit as meaningful and memorable. Just as poetry can express volumes in a few words, proposing the right toast at a right moment can be a significant, and important, gesture.

Because toasts are generally short, they are easy to remember or read. In addition, because they are a means of expressing wishes and feelings, rather than a theory or a discovery, you don't need to be an authority or expert to deliver a toast. You just need to be yourself.

Toasts also have the advantage of being delivered, and heard, live. Putting your feelings in writing can be much harder than speaking them. I was on the solicited freelance roster for American Greetings for a while and discovered that I had to write hundreds of cards for each one that was accepted. People often look for originality in print, but in toasts, all they ask for is sincerity. Using the same toast that your grandfather proposed at every family wedding is not only acceptable, it can be a moving tribute and tradition. Quoting the words of an author in a toast indicates that you are witty and well read.

Once you become adept at toasting, you'll find that there are countless occasions at which toasts are appropriate. Some of my friends toast at every meal. Their daily orange juice toast to toast may not be tremendously original, but it's not bad for 6:45 in the morning.

This book is designed to help you find toasts in a hurry when you need them. That's why it is divided into categories that give you specific toasts for specific occasions or people.

A few toasts appear in more than one chapter or section. This is because readers have told me that they often consult my books at the last possible moment when they have little time to skip throughout the text looking for witty words. In some cases, you will also find toasts that are very similar to each other. As toasts move from location to location, and generation to generation, variations develop. Try saying both versions out loud, and choose the one that feels the most natural to say.

The toasts in this book are just a starting point. I encourage you to change them in any way that seems right for the moment. You can often combine two short toasts together with the word "and" to make a longer toast.

When I know who originally uttered a thought that's in a toast, I tend to include that information. You can, for example, find this toast in the book:

> *"Here's to our new neighbors. It's clear that you know what Franklin P. Jones said: 'Nothing makes you more tolerant of a neighbor's party than being there.'"*

However, you may prefer to eliminate the name and just say

> *"Here's to our new neighbors. It's clear that you know that 'Nothing makes you more tolerant of a neighbor's party than being there.'"*

While this book's first purpose is to be an effective last-minute resource, I encourage you to also take a leisurely read through the whole book when you can. Reading toasts is fun, and once you know a few, you are likely to find opportunities to use them.

Cheers!

Chapter 1:

About Toasting

Proposing your toast

*I*f you are giving the first toast of the event, it's your job to instruct everyone in toasting. Stand up. Raise your glass high and say "Ladies and gentlemen, please raise your glasses in a toast in honor of _____." After that, people will generally have the idea, and all anyone has to say is "Let's toast to," "Here's to," "To _____," or some similar phrase.

In most situations, there's no need for phrases like "Drain your glasses." There are some cultures where the custom is that you must drink a whole container at each toast. They tend to use small cups. But in most cases, it is perfectly appropriate to just take a sip so you have room to participate in more toasts. Incidentally, if someone serves you champagne in a glass that has a stem but no base, that's a sign that they expect you to drink it all at once; the glass has been designed (or modified) so you can't put it down. For the record, I don't approve of those glasses. In addition to being an environmental nightmare, they often lead to spills, broken glass and puncture wounds.

Getting attention

If you are having trouble getting people's attention and you want to give a toast, it's okay to clink a piece of silverware against a glass to get everyone to turn to you. But, before you do so, ask yourself whether it might not be better to let people go on carousing for a while without interruption. Don't try to get attention by running a wet finger around the rim of your crystal goblet. You may get attention, but for the rest of the occasion, all of the kids who have seen this stunt for the first time will be trying it, and those who are hearing impaired will be busy attempting to adjust their hearing aids.

When you are giving a toast, don't make a big deal out of waiting for complete silence in the room, or waiting for everyone to have perfectly-filled glasses. Also, don't make a fuss if someone toasts with a glass of water; it's now considered perfectly appropriate to do so.

Danger: flying glasses

Despite what you've seen in movies, never start, and try to avoid, the business of toasting and then throwing the glass into the fireplace or the beer bottle against the wall. Sooner or later, someone gets cut. For the record, the custom of flinging glassware supposedly indicates that the toast that was just given was so sacred and profound that the glass should never be used for anything else again. If you really feel that way, put the glass away in a trunk in the attic with a tag on it.

To clink or not to clink

Once a toast is given, raise your glass and drink. If everyone else is clinking glasses, join in (gently, please.). One legend is that clinking is meant to make liquid from one glass slosh out into the next glass so that no one would be tempted to poison a glass. (If the idea of poisoning a glass seems tempting to you, rent the 1956 Danny Kaye movie, *The Court Jester*, to learn just how complicated it can get.) A different legend for the origin of glass clinking says that it is meant to make a bell-like chiming sound to scare off evil spirits who might be lurking in the fluid about to be consumed. The idea of evil spirits in alcohol makes intuitive sense to anyone who has ever gotten foolishly drunk or has been painfully hung over, but science has come up with more chemical explanations. If no one else starts the clinking business, we advise you to keep your glass to yourself.

A few handy toasting phrases

A health to . . .
Drain your glasses for . . .
Glasses off the table for . . .
Good luck to . . .
Here's luck to . . .
Here's to . . .
I give you . . .
I wish you . . .
Join me in saluting . . .
Let us all agree that . . .
Let's drink to . . .
Please assist me in expressing our love for . . .
Raise a glass to . . .
Raise your glasses to . . .
These blessings upon you . . .
Will you please be upstanding and drink, with me, a toast to . . .

How long should a toast be?

Once upon a time, toasts were longer. If you read accounts of Eighteenth Century banquets, you will find comments about flowery, 20-minute or longer toasts. Don't even think about rambling on for that long. Think of your toast as a commercial. Thirty seconds or so is a nice length. If you go on for much longer, people are likely to put their glasses down, or start drinking from them.

Being toasted

When you are being toasted, you should not drink. If you are thirsty, propose a toast to someone or something other than yourself, or take a sip between toasts.

Where does toasting come from?

There are many theories about where the custom of toasting comes from. The ancient Greeks and Romans drank to their gods. Then, again, their rulers sometimes wanted to be considered god-like, so they probably got toasted, too. Perhaps toasting started, and has survived, because it's a way of showing allegiance.

Drinking from a common source is also a way of showing that a person is welcome, and that the liquid is not poisoned. So perhaps toasting began, and is still with us, because it's such a natural way to demonstrate hospitality and trust.

However, my favorite theory is that the reason people have always toasted, and will always toast, is that it's fun and sociable.

Where does the word 'toast' come from?

In ancient times, the wine making process was not as scientific and perfect as it is today. When we uncork a bottle today, we are reasonably sure it'll be tasty. But in the days before stainless steel vats and temperature controlled buildings (not to mention obscure additives and processes), wine could often become quite acidic. Throwing a bit of toasted bread into the wine was a primitive form of charcoal filtering. The toast might absorb some of the impurities and could balance the chemistry of the brew. Somewhere along the line, the idea of draining a glass came to be described as drinking a toast.

There's a related story about a woman bathing in the baths at Bath, England, in 1709, whose beauty was so inspiring that an awed young man offered to drink the bathwater. In some versions of the tale, people threw toast into the bathwater and a man offered to eat it. The stories seem to be a bit odd, until you think of them in the context of modern bragging compliments and factor in the odds that the accounts we were told in school might have underplayed the sexual tone of the comments. In effect, the comment was probably the equivalent of "she looks good enough to eat" or "she's so fine I'd walk across a mile of broken glass in my bare feet just to sniff her laundry." Whatever the story, drinking a toast was established as a way to salute someone's beauty.

How toasting is changing

Toasts are getting shorter. That's a good thing. Toasts used to go on forever. There are records of toasts that went on for hours and then, of course, people would respond at equal length.

For example, this book suggests that you toast a baby using Mark Twain's comment, "We haven't all had the good fortune to be ladies, we haven't all been generals or poets or statesmen; but when the toast works down to babies, we stand on common ground." But when Twain first made that witty remark, it was part of a long toast at a dinner in honor of General Grant. Twain was, by reputation, a great speaker, and his toast contained many witty words, such as "twins amount to a permanent riot," but it still must have seemed long.

Another change is that today there are generally fewer toasts given at an occasion than in the past. Twain's toast was the fifteenth formal toast at that dinner. In England at more formal occasions, there was an established order in which toasts should be given. The first toast was to the king or queen. Then toasts were given to various branches of the military, judges, ministers, etc.

Today's toasts *are* shorter and fewer, but perhaps more sincere. People are much more interested in hearing you say something about someone you know and care deeply about, than in hearing you pledge fealty to an official of some sort or another. For example, Robert Redford gave a toast to "Healing the Earth" at a conference. It's a perfect modern toast: It expresses admiration and allegiance, it's short and sincere, it expresses a wish, and tells you something about the person making the wish.

A Toast to the Reader

Here's to toasting.
May you enjoy it
as much as I do.

Chapter 2

Words for Weddings

$\mathcal{W}$eddings, and the various occasions that surround them, are the occasions at which we hear, and give, the most toasts. This chapter provides toasts you could use at:

- ❧ Engagement Parties.
- ❧ Wedding Showers.
- ❧ Bachelor Parties.
- ❧ Bachelorette Parties.
- ❧ Rehearsal Dinners.
- ❧ Wedding Receptions.

Toasts for Anniversaries and Divorces are found in Special Occasions (Chapter 3).

Engagement Party

Engagements are traditionally announced by the father of the bride with an appropriate toast, but that's just a tradition, and a hard one to pull off, at that. In many cases, the groom no longer asks the bride's father for permission to pop the question, and the bride's father may be one of the last to know, rather than one of the first.

Here's to the ring.

"To every lovely lady bright,
I wish a gallant faithful knight;
To every faithful lover, too,
I wish a trusting lady true."
—Sir Walter Scott

As Mark Twain said, "To get the full value of joy,
you must have someone to divide it with."

"Here's looking at you, kid."
—Humphrey Bogart toasting Ingrid Bergman in *Casablanca*

Wedding Shower

Wedding showers happen between the engagement party and the wedding, and, in most cases, before the baby shower. No one takes a shower at these events; the bride, or the couple, gets showered with gifts, and, perhaps, toasts.

Here's to the happy couple:
May you survive your wedding and still be in love.

In the words of Ralph Waldo Emerson, "All the world loves a lover."

Here's to the bride that is to be,
Happy and smiling and fair.
And here's to those who would like to be,
And are wondering when, and where.

Here's to matrimony:
The high sea for which no compass has yet been invented.

Bachelor Party

Bachelor parties are one of the ultimate toasting occasions. Traditionally, they are the bachelor's last completely rowdy night out with the boys. This, of course, is nonsense since many of the guests at a bachelor party are married men. In recent years, there has been a trend in which the bride and her bridesmaids join the bachelor party, presumably to critique any strippers who might happen to show up or to be on hand in case anyone has to post bail. The toasts below are relatively sedate compared to some of what you may hear at a bachelor blowout.

To quote Jonathan Brown, and the bachelor's girlfriends, "Whenever the occasion arose, he rose to the occasion."

Here's to old wine and young women.
Needles and pins, needles and pins.
When a man marries his troubles begin.

Here's to the women that I've loved and all the ones I've kissed.
As for regrets, I just have one; that's all the ones I've missed.

Oh, womens' faults are many, we men have only two:
Every single thing we say, and everything we do.

Drink, my buddies, drink with discerning,
Wedlock's a lane where there is no turning;
Never was owl more blind than lover;
Drink and be merry, lads; and think it over.

Say it with flowers,
Say it with eats,
Say it with kisses,
Say it with sweets,
Say it with jewelry,
Say it with drink,
But always be careful
Not to say it with ink.

To the bachelor:
A man who refuses to play troth or consequences.

To the bachelor:
A man who can have a girl on his knees without having her on his hands.

To the bachelor, who, as Helen Rowland once remarked, "never quite gets over the idea that he is a thing of beauty and a boy forever."

To the wisdom of the bachelor:
To quote H.L. Mencken, he "knows more about women than married men; if he didn't, he'd be married too."

"Marriage is a wonderful institution, but who wants to live in an institution?"
—Groucho Marx

In the words of Minna Thomas Antrim,
"Drink, for who knows when Cupid's arrow keen,
Shall strike us and no more we'll here be seen."

To men—the bitter half of women.

To the bachelors:
May they never impale their freedom upon the point of a pen.

A game, a book, a fire, a friend,
A beer that's always full,
Here's to the joys of a bachelor's life,
A life that's never dull.

To marriage:
An institution very much like a tourniquet because it stops your circulation.

To marriage:
The last decision a man is allowed to make.

"I have a dozen healths,
To drink to these fair ladies."
—Shakespeare, *Henry VIII*

Here's to women, the sweethearts, the wives,
The delights of our firesides by night and by day,
Who never do anything wrong in their lives,
Except when permitted to have their own way.

Let her be clumsy, or let her be slim,
Young or ancient, I care not a feather;

So fill up a goblet, fill it to the brim,
Let us toast all the ladies together.

As the song goes, "Another one bites the dust."

"Drink to fair woman, whom, I think,
Is most entitled to it,
For if anything ever can drive me to drink,
She certainly could do it."
—B. Jabez Jenkins

Fee-simple and the simple fee,
And all the fees in tail
Are nothing when compared with thee,
Thou best of fees—fee-male.

Bachelorette Party

I don't know a lot about these parties, having always been told I was not welcome and wouldn't enjoy them anyway. I have heard rumors, however, that they are very similar to bachelor parties in tone and spirit.

Here's to the men, God bless them!
Worst of my sins, I confess them!
In loving them all, be they great or small,
So here's to the boys! God bless them!

Here's to the men we love.
Here's to the men that love us.
Here's to the men we love, but don't love us.
Oh, screw them, let's drink to us.

May your wedding night be like a kitchen table...
all legs and no drawers.

Here's to the bachelorette:
She looks but she won't leap.

To the bachelorette:
A woman who hasn't made the same mistake once.

Oh, here's to the good and the bad men, too,
For without them saints would have nothing to do!

Oh, I love them both, and I love them well,
But which I love better, I never can tell!

May all single men get married,
and all married men be happy.

Here's to the man who is wisest and best,
Here's to the man with judgment is blest.
Here's to the man who's as smart as can be—
I mean the man who agrees with me.

Here's to our friend finding a guy with a pierced ear. As Rita
Rudner says, "I think men who have a pierced ear are better
prepared for marriage. They've experienced pain and bought
jewelry."

To men:
They divide our time, double our cares, and triple our troubles.

To men—creatures who buy playoff tickets months in advance
and wait until Christmas Eve to buy presents.

To the two things that delight a young girl's heart:
Fresh flowers and fresh men!

Here's to the men of all classes
Who through lasses and glasses
Will make themselves asses!

"Man is the only animal who laughs, drinks when he is not thirsty,
and makes love at all seasons of the year."
—Voltaire

Women's faults are many,
Men have only two—
Everything they say,
And everything they do.

Here's to the fellow who smiles,
While life rolls on like a song,
But here's to the chap who can smile,
When everything goes dead wrong.

Here's to the gentlemen—first in our hearts and first in our pants.

Women, beware of men! To quote an old song "Frankie and Johnnie,"
"This story has no moral,
This story has no end,
This story only goes to show
That there ain't no good in men.
They'll do you wrong just as sure's you're born."

Rehearsal Dinner

If a couple is having a large wedding, there may be so many people at the reception that there are few opportunities for toasting. People could be filtering through the reception line for hours, and the exhausted couple may be kidnapped by the photographer who wants to get some shots of them outside while the light is perfect. In those instances, you might prefer to do your toasting at the rehearsal dinner where there are fewer people.

While the rehearsal dinner occurs before the wedding just like the Bachelor and Bachelorette parties, the toasts are closer to wedding toasts in tone. This is the place to make toasts about family and about the joining of families. One trick is to use the couple's names in a toast. When my cousin, Betty Pinkham, married Alan Anderson many years ago, I proposed a toast "to the Anderhams," at the rehearsal dinner which was packed with Pinkhams and Andersons. They remember the toast fondly and bring it up almost every time I see them.

Often, the bride's parents start the toasting at this meal because the groom's family is paying for the drinks, while the bride's parents are more likely to be picking up the tab at the wedding. Almost any toast that can be used at a wedding can be used at the rehearsal dinner.

Here's to you and yours
And to mine and ours.
And if mine and ours
Ever come across to you and yours,
I hope you and yours will do
As much for mine and ours
As mine and ours have done
For you and yours!

Here's a health to all those that we love,
Here's a health to all those that love us,
Here's a health to all those that love them
that love those
that love them
that love those
that love us.

Here's my advice to the happy couple:
Dance as if no one were watching,
Sing as if no one were listening,
And live every day as if it were your last.

May you have many children;
and may they grow as mature in taste,
and as healthy in color,
and as sought after
as the contents of this glass.

May your wedding days be few and your anniversaries many.

Wedding Reception

Who Gives the First Toast?

There are hundreds of books on the etiquette of wedding celebrations that make definitive statements about who proposes the first, second, and third toast and to whom the toasts are dedicated. You can read them if you want to, but the bottom line on the situation is that you should do what the bride wants you to do at wedding celebrations, except, perhaps, the bachelor party. In some cases, the groom's or the bride's mother has some say in the matter, but the bride's wishes trump everything else. If she wants one of her sorority sisters who didn't get to be a bridesmaid to have the first toast privilege, that's how it should be.

If the bride and groom are too busy with other things to care, the person hosting (or paying for) the event can claim the privilege, except at the wedding itself, where the first toast is technically one of the duties of the bestman. Traditionally, that means the father of the bride gives the toast at the engagement party, and the father of the groom gives the first toast at the rehearsal party.

These rules make little sense when the bride and groom are paying for their own wedding and can actually get a bit problematic when the bride's father is splitting the cost with his ex-wife and her current husband. In some cases, the answer is to have several people get up together and propose a joint toast. In others, the best move may be to have the first toast given by a precocious 12-year-old whose glass is filled with ginger ale.

If you are really set on following a traditional toasting sequence at a wedding, it generally goes something like this:

1. Bestman.
2. Groom's Father.
3. Bride's Father.
4. Groom.
5. Bride.
6. Maid of Honor.
7. Groom's Mother.
8. Bride's Mother.

Of course, many people today object to the idea of letting the first four toasts be given by men, so an alternative sequence that some couples are using goes:

1. Bestman.
2. Maid of Honor.
3. Groom's Parents.
4. Bride's Parents.
5. Friends.

It's easy to see how this gets complicated when there are multiple sets of parents. So, once again, our advice is to let the bride set the sequence that she feels is right.

To Whom and to What You Toast

Your toast is to the bride, or the bride and groom, and about their happiness. If you understand that, you can skip the next few paragraphs. If you are tempted to make your toast to anything other than the bride or the couple, read on.

Your toast is not about the bride's grandmother or any other member of the family, dead or alive. Avoid the temptation to tell the bride that, at that moment, your heart is filled with the sense that dear departed Nona is smiling down on the room from heaven, even if they didn't let you hang the oil painting portrait of her over the table with the book that guests should sign. I was there when that toast was delivered. The bride started crying and the whole room took a while to recover. That message could have been delivered privately, after the occasion. *The toast is about the bride and groom.*

The toast is not about how the wedding would have been even grander if the bride's father was not such a deadbeat. I was there when a bride's mother, in a low-cut red dress that screamed for attention, delivered just such a toast. The bride, I hear, didn't speak to her mother for a month.

Your toast is not about the fact that the joyous union of these people represents another victory for your culture, race, nationality, etc. (Unless, of course, this is an arranged marriage and that is the sole reason the couple was brought together.) *The toast is about the bride and groom.*

Your toast is not to the children the couple may some day have. You don't know whether or not the couple can get pregnant. You don't know if they want to get pregnant. You don't know if they were pregnant and lost the child. Even if you do know any of this, act as if you don't know it at the wedding. *The toast is about the bride and groom.* A possible exception to this is that, if the bride has given ample signals that this is how she feels, the toast can be about the bride, groom and a child or children that either of them already has. When in doubt, you guessed it, *the toast is about the bride and groom.*

ɜ A Special Note to Bestmen ɕ

By the time the best man gets around to giving his toast at the reception, the wedding process is in the home stretch. The showers, the bachelor party and even the wedding have been survived. There is a natural temptation to loosen up a bit. Don't do it. Keep the toast about the bride and groom and their happiness.

Your toast is not about why you were chosen bestman. The fact that you bailed the groom out after that hilarious encounter with the transvestite at Mardi Gras is *not* relevant to this situation.

The toast is not about how great the bachelor party was. The temptation to talk about this must be very strong, because I have heard many bestmen bring this topic up. Keep the fact that you find it amazing that the groom is able to look so good just a few days after slurping so many Jello shots out of the navels of the fabulous dancing Martinez twins to yourself.

The toast is not about your speculations as to what could happen on the honeymoon, or how much trouble you went to arrange for a bungalow for them in Mexico that has mirrors on the ceiling.

The best way to be a best man is to keep it short and sweet. The one big exception here is what I call the "kamikaze decoy best man." If the bride and groom indicate to you that they are overwhelmed (first warning sign: one of them can't stop crying), you can use your toast to stall so they have time to recover. Again, this is not a moment to tell tales. One tactic is to call on people around the room, one at a time, by name, and ask them to stand and join you in extending your best wishes.

ɜ A Special Note to Bridesmaids ɕ

Your toast is not about the strange dress that the bride made you, as a bridesmaid, buy and wear.

The toast is certainly not about you. If, when you are practicing your toast, you hear yourself say "I," "me," or "we" three or more times, stop and think of a new toast. If you find yourself saying *you* always knew she would find someone wonderful and how *you* picked berries together in Blue Hill when *you* were three and how *you* hope she finds the same happiness that *you* have with *your* wonderful spouse, there's too much you in it. The toast is also not about the wonderful gift you are giving the couple. That's just another way of talking about you. *The toast is to and about the bride or about the bride and groom. It is, in essence, a Best Wishes toast.*

If you are still tempted to mention yourself or people other than the bride and groom in your toast, rent the movie *Four Weddings and a Funeral* and watch as a guest toasts the groom for winning such a lovely bride (so far so good) but also mentions that his other girlfriends (some of whom are in attendance) had been complete "dogs." Not only will a comment like that ruin your chances of getting a date with the grooms-men, it could also be the cause of the newly married couple's first argument.

May there always be work for your hands to do.
May your purse always hold a coin or two.
May the sun always shine warm on your windowpane.
May a rainbow be certain to follow each rain.
May the hand of a friend always be near you.
And may God fill your heart with gladness to cheer you.

May you both live as long as you want,
And never want as long as you live.

May your glasses be ever full,
May the roof over your heads be always strong,
And may you be in heaven half an hour
Before the devil knows you're dead.

May you be poor in misfortune,
Rich in blessings,
Slow to make enemies,
And quick to make friends.

As you slide down the bannister of life,
May the splinters never point the wrong way.

May the joys of today
Be those of tomorrow.
The goblets of life
Hold no dregs of sorrow.

May the saddest day of your future be no worse
Than the happiest day of your past.

May you have many children
and may they grow as mature in taste,
and as healthy in color,
and as sought after
as the contents of this glass.

May the most you wish for
Be the least you get.

May your troubles be less
And your blessings be more.
And nothing but happiness
Come through your door.

May the blessings of light be upon you,
Light without and light within.
And in all your comings and goings,
May you ever have a kindly greeting
From them you meet along the road.

May brooks and trees and singing hills
Join in the chorus, too.
And every gentle wind that blows
Send happiness to you.

May you have food and raiment,
A soft pillow for your head,
May you be forty years in heaven
Before the devil knows you're dead.

May there be a generation of children
On the children of your children.

May all your ups and downs
come only in the bedroom.

Here's to the bride and the bridegroom:
We'll ask their success in our prayers,
And through life's dark shadows and sunshine
That good luck may always be theirs.

Let's drink to the health of the bride,
Let's drink to the health of the groom,

Let's drink to the Parson who tied,
And to every guest in the room!

Here's to thee and thy folks from me and my folks;
And if thee and thy folks love me and my folks
As much as me and my folks love thee and thy folks
Then there never was folks since folks was folks
Love me and my folks as much as thee and thy folks.

In the immortal words of Ralph Waldo Emerson, "Here's to the happy man: All the world loves a lover."

Here's to the groom with bride so fair,
And here's to the bride with groom so rare!

To the man who has conquered the bride's heart, and her mother's.

Here's to the new husband and here's to the new wife:
May they remain lovers for all of life.

Here's to the Bride and the Groom!
May you have a happy honeymoon,
May you lead a happy life,
May you make a bunch of money soon,
And live without all strife.

Here's to the bride:
Anna Lewis said it best when she wrote,
"Love, be true to her; Life, be dear to her;
Health, stay close to her; Joy, draw near to her;
Fortune, find what you can do for her,
Search your treasure-house through and through for her,
Follow her footsteps the wide world over,
And keep her husband always her lover."

Here's to the bride:
May your hours of joy be as numerous as the petals of your bridal bouquet.

Here's to our groom:
A man who keeps his head though he loses his heart.

Here's to the man whose best girl is his mother, and whose sweetheart is his wife.

A toast to the groom—and discretion to his bachelor friends.

May all your joys be pure joys,
and all your pain, champagne.

I wish you health, I wish you well,
And happiness galore.
I wish you luck for you and friends;
What could I wish you more?

May your joys be as deep as the oceans,
Your troubles as light as its foam.
And may you find, sweet peace of mind,
Wherever you may roam.

May you taste the sweetest pleasures
That fortune ere bestowed,
And may all your friends remember
All the favors you are owed.

Happiness being a dessert so sweet
May life give you more than you can ever eat.

May your laugh, your love, and your wine be plenty,
thus your happiness will be nothing less.

When the roaring flames of your love have burned down to embers, may you find that you've married your best friend.

May your home always be too small to hold all your friends.

To marriage:
The happy estate which, as Sydney Smith observed, "resembles a pair of shears; so joined that they cannot be separated; often moving in opposite directions, yet always punishing anyone who comes between them."

May all single men get married,
and all married men be happy.

To the wonderful institution called marriage:
It's one of the few relationships where, as Elbert Hubbard said,
"Man's boldness and woman's caution make an excellent business
arrangement."

To a happy marriage, or in the words of Andre Maurois, "to a
long conversation that always seems too short."

May their joys be as deep as the ocean
And their misfortunes as light as the foam.

May you grow old on one pillow.

May your love be as endless as your wedding rings.

Parents' toast: "It is written: when children find true love, parents
find true joy." Here's to your joy and ours, from this day forward.

Here's a toast to love and laughter
and happily ever after.

These two, now standing hand in hand,
Remind us of our native land,
For when today they linked their fates,
They entered the United States.

Here's to the bride
And here's to the groom
And to the bride's father
Who'll pay for this room.

To quote Walter Winchell, "Never above you. Never below you.
Always beside you."

Down the hatch, to a striking match.

Here's to the bride and the mother-in-law,
Here's to the groom and the father-in-law,
Here's to the sister and brother-in-law,
Here's to friends and friends-in-law,
May none of you need an attorney-at-law.

To marriage, which Ambrose Bierce defined as "A community
consisting of a master, a mistress, and two slaves, making in all, two.

To the happy couple:
May all your troubles be little ones.

As Shakespeare said in *Romeo and Juliet,*
may "a flock of blessings light upon thy back."

"Look down you gods,
and on this couple drop a blessed crown."
—Shakespeare, *Tempest*

Here's to my mother-in-law's daughter,
Here's to her father-in-law's son;
Here's to the vows we've just taken,
And the life we've just begun.

Here's to this fine couple:
May their joys be as bright as the
morning, and their sorrows but
shadows that fade in the sunlight of
love.

While there's life on the lip,
While there's warmth in the wine,
One deep health I'll pledge,
And that health shall be thine.

May we all have the unspeakable good fortune to win a true
heart, and the merit to keep it.

To love, or as Martin Tupper once said, "Love—what a volume in
a word, an ocean in a tear!"

May those now love
Who never loved before;
May those who've loved
Now love the more.

A thousand welcomes you will find here before you,
And the oftener you come here the more I'll adore you.

Because I love you truly,
Because you love me, too,

My very greatest happiness
Is sharing life with you.

Here's to one and only one,
And may that one be he
Who loves but one and only one,
And may that one be me.

Here's to you who halves my sorrows and doubles my joys.

I love you more than yesterday, less than tomorrow.

May we love as long as we live, and live as long as we love.

May we have those in our arms that we love in our hearts.

To the wings of love:
May they never lose a feather,
But soar up to the sky above,
And last and last forever.

Here's to my sweetheart's eyes,
Those homes of emotion.
Oh, how they make me think.
I like them sad.
I prefer them glad.
But I love them when they wink.

I have known many,
Liked a few,
Loved one.
Here's to you.

Here's to love:
The only fire against which there is no insurance.

To love:
Dorothy Parker described it as the "quicksilver in the hand.
Leave the fingers open and it stays in the palm; clutch it and it
darts away."

Thou hast no faults, or no faults I can spy;
Thou art all beauty, or all blindness I.

To quote Elbert Hubbard, "The love you give away is the only love you keep."

To moderation in all things—except in love.

Here's to the red and sparkling wine,
I'll be your sweetheart, if you'll be mine.
I'll be constant, I'll be true,
I'll leave my happy home for you.

The world is filled with flowers,
The flowers filled with dew,
The dew is filled with love
For you, and you, and you.

May your love be like good wine, and grow
stronger as it grows older.

(Parent to new in-law)
I toast you from my heart.
I toast you with my spouse.
We're glad you married our child
Who will finally get out of the house.

To the happy couple:
May you find that love not only makes the world go 'round, it makes the trip worthwhile.

Here's to the girl I love and
Here's to the girl who loves me.
Here's to those who love the girl I love,
And, all those who love the girl I love who love me.

May you live all the years of your life.
—Jonathan Swift

May the best day of your past be the worst day of your future.

May you look back fifty years from now and agree that today was the worst day of your married life.

To the bridesmaids:
We admire them for their beauty, respect them for their

intelligence, adore them for their virtues, and love them because we can't help it.

Let anniversaries come and let anniversaries go
but may your happiness continue on forever.

May your nets always be full,
Your pockets never empty.
May your horse not cast a shoe
Or the devil look at you
In the year that lies ahead!

Gay/Lesbian/Transgendered Marriages/ Commitment Ceremonies

The idea that you need different toasts for gay marriages is a bit silly. Love is love. But there are many old toasts with the word "gay" that are fun because they have taken on new meaning. Some people also appreciate toasts written by authors who are or were gay.

Let's be gay while we may
And seize love with laughter:
I'll be true as long as you,
But not a moment after.

May you live as long as you want to.
And may you want to as long as you live.

Let's drink to love,
Which is nothing
Unless it's divided by two.

In the words of James Keene, "Here's to those who love us well— those who don't may go to Hell."

Love to one, friendship to a few, and goodwill to all.

To the life we love with those we love.

May we be loved by those we love.

May we kiss those we please, and please those we kiss.

Second/Third/Fourth Marriages

No matter how many times a person has been married, it is generally best to treat the marriage like it is a first marriage. That means that you can use almost any marriage toast.

Rich or poor, quick or slow,
May you know nothing but happiness
From this day forward.

Here's to lasses we've loved,
Here's to the lips we've pressed;
For of kisses and lasses,
Like liquor and glasses,
The last is always the best.

To a second marriage:
Which Samuel Johnson described as "the triumph of hope over experience."

Typical of my friend, third time's a charm.

I toast you for doing what we were always told to do: Try, try again.

When the flaming love you now know
Takes on a calmer glow,
May you find, in the end,
That you married a best friend.

Older Marriages

Unless you have very clear indications that the bride wants to be thought of as an older bride, you should treat an older marriage the same way you would a marriage of teenagers and use one of the earlier toasts.

May you see each other through any dark days,
and make all the rest a little brighter.

May you have warm words on a cold evening,
A full moon on a dark night,
And the road downhill all the way to your door.

To all your days now and after:
May they be filled with fond memories, happiness, and laughter.

Grow old with me! The best is yet to be,
The last of life, for which, the first is made.
—Robert Browning

A Toast to the Reader

May the high point
Of a day people wed
Be a witty toast—
The one you said!

Chapter 3
Toasts for Special Occasions

*Y*ou don't need to have a special occasion for toasting, but many occasions seem to call for toasts to commemorate the moment. If you don't find the perfect toast for an occasion below, check the toasts in Best Wishes (Chapter 5).

Adult Education Graduation

It takes a particular courage and endurance to be able to attend school as an adult. When someone graduates, it's time for toasting.

In the Fifth century B.C., Confucius complained that, "In old days men studied for the sake of self-improvement; nowadays men study in order to impress other people." It's working. I'm impressed.

Aeschylus said, "It is always the season for the old to learn." Here's to students of all ages.

Peter Ustinov said, "I am convinced that it is of primordial importance to learn more every year than the year before. After all, what is education but a process by which a person begins to learn how to learn." He's right, and you're all proof of that. Here's to you.

Anniversary

Since an anniversary is a celebration of a wedding, you can use almost every toast in the Wedding Reception section of Wedding Toasts (Chapter 2) at an anniversary party.

Here's to the husband
And here's to the wife;
May they remain
Lovers for life.

May their joys be as deep as the ocean
And their misfortunes as light as the foam.
May you grow old on one pillow.

May your love be as endless as your wedding rings.

To my spouse:
Here's a health to the future,
A sigh for the past,
We can love and remember
And love to the last.

To my wife and our anniversary, which I forgot once, but will never forget again.

Here's to you both
A beautiful pair,
On the birthday of
Your love affair.

To the happy couple:
Let anniversaries come and let anniversaries go but may your happiness continue on forever.

To your coming anniversaries:
May they be outnumbered only by your coming pleasures.

To my spouse:
Because I love you truly,
Because you love me, too,
My very greatest happiness
Is sharing life with you.

To a couple so happy they raise the same question in all of our minds: "Are you sure they're married?"

To my parents' anniversary, that most important day, which proves that I am, after all, legitimate.

To my wife:
The reason for my life,
My bride and joy.

April Fools' Day

When giving or responding to a toast on April Fools' Day, check your glass carefully. Some of us have been known to find "dribble glasses" funny or to mix drinks with salt instead of sugar.

Here's to the jokers:
Who do their worst
Every year
On April first.

"Let us toast the fools; but for them, the rest of us could not succeed."
—Mark Twain

To April Fools' Day, the most honest day of the year.

May the skepticism that we develop on April Fools' Day protect us for the rest of the year.

May the pranks we fall for today be the only ones we fall for all year.

Art Opening and Exhibit

For many of us, art openings are challenging events at which to speak. Artists and art critics seem to have a language all their own, and some of the comments we might intend as compliments can be taken as evidence of ignorance, or even criticism. The solution, of course, is to give a toast in which you talk about the nature of art, or the courage of artists, while avoiding passing judgment on the works that are being shown.

Here's to art:
As G. K. Chesterton once said so eloquently, "Art, like morality, consists in drawing the line somewhere."

To art:
As George Bernard Shaw said, "Without art, the crudeness of reality would make the world unbearable."

To art, that which distinguishes man from beast.

To art:
May we all serve it.

To art, which demands all our energy. To quote Ralph Waldo Emerson, "Art is a jealous mistress."

Ben Jonson said, "Art has an enemy called ignorance." Here's to the triumph of art and the end to ignorance.

As Victor Cousin said, "Art for art's sake."

Award Presentation

If you are the toastee, the person who is being praised for having won the award, it's usually enough to just smile and say "thank you." If, however, the toasting gets out of hand and you want to slow things down a bit, you can always use the tried-and-true line, "you people are toasting me so much I feel like a loaf of bread."

In *The Apocrypha* it says "Let us now praise famous men," so let's get to it with a drink to our new star.

To our winner:
Napoleon Bonaparte said, "Great men are meteors designed to burn so that the earth may be lighted." Thank you for your brightness.

To a very determined man:
Charles de Gaulle said, "Nothing great will ever be achieved without great men, and men are great only if they are determined to be so." He could have been describing you.

Winston Churchill said, "Meeting Franklin Roosevelt was like opening your first bottle of champagne; knowing him was like drinking it." I could say the same about you. Here's to how you sparkle.

Benjamin Franklin said "Well done is better than well said," and all I can say about your accomplishments is well done. Here's to you!

Baby Shower

Baby showers are misnamed. There are generally no babies there (they show up a while later) and no showering happens. There is, often, an odd ritual that involves making a hat out of the ribbons that came on the gift packages and demanding that the showeree wear them, but that's another story. If you're lucky, there's some toasting to the mom, or perhaps the couple, who are expecting.

"We haven't all had the good fortune to be ladies, we haven't all been generals or poets or statesmen; but when the toast works down to babies, we stand on common ground."
—Mark Twain

To your baby:
May the child make your love stronger, days shorter, nights longer, bankroll smaller, home happier, clothes shabbier, past forgotten, and the future worth living for.

To the expected blessed event:
This will mean a change for you. In fact, it will mean many changes

To you:
You don't know what you're getting into!

Here's to the baby,
Man to be,
May he be as fine as thee.

Here's to baby,
Woman to be,
May she be as sweet as thee.

May your baby grow twice as tall as you and half as wise.

"Every baby born into the world is a finer one than the last."
—Charles Dickens

A new life begun,
Like father, like son.

Like one, like the other,
Like daughter, like mother.

To the new parents:
They will learn, as I did, about babies, that you've got to love them. Unfortunately, you also have to feed them and change them, too. Good luck!

To the new baby, who, as the parents will soon find out, is the perfect example of minority rule.

As they say in the diaper business, bottoms up!

Banquet

In a formal banquet where there is a dais (a raised platform where all the VIPs are seated), you should only propose a toast if you are one of those chosen to be on the dais. In a less formal banquet where everyone sits on the same level, you can propose a toast at any time after the host has made the first toast. Often, you can propose a toast to the group that is holding the banquet. "Here's to the Daughters of Scotia and all they do to keep our traditions alive." When in doubt, you can always toast the idea of having a banquet.

When you give a toast at a banquet, be sure to indicate who you want to join you. If you are proposing a toast that the whole room should join in on, stand up and make an attempt to get everyone's attention. If your toast is just intended for your tablemates, it may be best to remain seated.

In *Ecclesiastes*, 9:10, it is written, "Eat thy bread with joy, and drink thy wine with a merry heart." Who are we to disobey? Here's to this feast; let's enjoy it."

To the good old days, which we are having right now.

As Baba Meher said, "Don't worry, be happy."

After everything that has happened, I can only quote the last words of Czar Alexander I of Russia, "What a beautiful day."

"Drink today and drown all sorrow,
You shall perhaps not do't tomorrow
Best while you have it, use your breath;
There is no drinking after death."
—Francis Beaumont & John Fletcher

I wish you all the best. As Shakespeare said in *Timon of Athens*, may "The best of happiness, honor and fortunes keep with you."

Happy are we met, happy have we been,
Happy may we part, and happy meet again.

Baptism/Christening

Many religions, sects and cultures have specific rituals in which a child is welcomed into the community. These are generally joyous occasions, and so naturally they are often celebrated with a friendly toast, and gifts. In more formal times, the godfather would propose a toast at a christening to "the little stranger" before the child had been christened. Then he would toast the health of the child, and affirm his sponsorship in a second toast. The child's father would then respond with a toast to the godparents. The godfather would, of course, respond with a toast thanking the father for his toast. We don't know of anyone who goes through all that today, but toasts still abound at these occasions.

Let's toast the stork that brought the baby. Everyone stand on one leg while they raise their glasses and take a drink!

May this be the last bath at which your baby cries.

In the words of Charles Dickens, "Every baby born into the world is a finer one than the last."

Let's wet our whistles. The baby will soon enough wet the rest of us.

A baby will make love stronger,
Days shorter, nights longer,
Bankroll smaller, home happier,
Clothes shabbier,
The past forgotten,
And the future worth living for.

A new life begun,
Like father, like son.

Like one, like the other,
Like daughter, like mother.

Here's to the baby
Man to be
May he be as fine as thee.

Here's to baby
Woman to be
May she be as sweet as thee.

[To the mother]
As Dorothy Parker once said to a friend who had just given birth, "Congratulations! We all knew you had it in you."

Bar Mitzvah/ Bat Mitzvah

Bar Mitzvahs and Bat Mitzvahs are coming-of-age-occasions much like Christian Confirmations. Almost any sincere toast in Best Wishes (Chapter 5) will be appropriate.

Here's to the parents! Well done!

L'chayim (To Life)!

Mazel tov (Congratulations)!

Bastille Day

July 14th is a great day to be French or to know someone who is French. Bastille Day is their Independence Day, and they tend to celebrate it with lots of toasting. You should, too. After all, thousands of French people aren't likely to be wrong.

Plus je bois, mieux je chante. (The more I drink, the better I sing.)

Lafayette, we are here!

A votre sante. (To your health.)

We'll always have Paris. Here's to us.

Sante (Health)!

Merde

Birthday

Almost any friendly toast is appropriate for a birthday, but here are a few favorites. If you don't find one that seems perfect for the moment below, check to see if there is something that feels right in Special People (Chapter 4) or in Best Wishes (Chapter 5).

Here's to you:
No matter how old you are, you don't look it.

Here's to you! No matter how old you are, you're still younger than I am.

To your birthday, glass held high,
Glad it's you that's older and not I.

To wish you joy on your birthday
And all the whole year through,
For all the best that life can hold
Is none too good for you.

On your birthday,
Glasses held high;
It's you that's aging;
It's certainly not I!

Happiness, being a dessert so sweet,
May life give you more than you can ever eat.

For the test of the heart is trouble
And it always comes with years.
And the smile that is worth the praises of earth
Is the smile that shines through the tears.

May all your joys be pure joys,
and all your pain champagne.

The test of gold is fire,
The test of truth is time,
The tests of God's love are the heavens above
And everything sublime.
Treasures in life are many;
Dreams realized but few
But I know the proof of God's goodness
Is that he gave me a friend like you.

A toast to your coffin:
May it be made of 100 year old oak
And may we plant the tree together, tomorrow.

May friendship, like wine, improve as time advances.
And may we always have old wine, old friends, and young cares.

May you taste the sweetest pleasures that fortune ere bestowed,
and may all your friends remember all the favors you are owed.

Here's to your aging:
As they say in Ireland,

"Twenty years a child;
Twenty years running wild;
Twenty years a mature man,
And after that, praying."

Since you are now a year older, I would like to remind you of
something a poet once said:
"You're not too old when your hair turns gray.
You're not too old when your teeth decay.
But you'll know you're awaiting that final sleep,
When your mind makes promises your body can't keep."
You're still a long way from that. Here's to you.

On your birthday,
Four blessings upon you:
Older whiskey,
Younger women,
Faster horses,
More money!
Cheers!

May you live to be a hundred years,
With one extra year to repent!

You're not as young as you used to be.
But, you're not as old as you're going to be.
So watch it!

On your birthday, I remind you of the wisdom of Groucho Marx,
who said, "A man is only as old as the woman he feels."

What is but Age? Something to count?
Some people fight it as if climbing the mount.
I choose live with dignity and grace
And offer a drink to all in this place!

To a grand old lady who has gotten better with age, I recite the
famous lyrics "The old gray mare ain't what she used to be."

To Age! To Age! Why does one care?
As the wrinkles grow longer and gray graces your hair.
Life should be simple because when push comes to shove,
The only one counting is the good Lord above!

May you die in bed at 95 years,
Shot by a jealous wife [husband]!

On your birthday, I offer you the words of a wise man:
"Do not resent growing old.
Many are denied the privilege."
Here's to you.

In the words of Jonathan Swift,
"May you live all the days of your life."
Cheers.

May there be a generation of children
On the children of your children.

Here's to a long life and a merry one.
A quick death and an easy one.
A pretty girl and an honest one.
A cold beer—and another one!

May I see you gray
And combing your grandchildren's hair.

Here are my birthday wishes for you:
May your liquor be cold,
May your women be hot,
And may your troubles slide off you
Slicker than snot.

I've drank to your health in taverns,
I've drank to your health in my home,
I've drank to your health so damn many times,
I believe I've ruined my own!

Another candle on your cake?
Well, that's no cause to pout.
Be glad that you have strength enough
To blow the damn thing out.

Another year older?
Think this way:
Just one day older
Than yesterday.

Happy birthday to you
And many to be,
With friends that are true
As you are to me.

In the words of Robert H. Lord,
"Many happy returns of the day of your birth:
Many blessings to brighten your pathway on earth;
Many friendships to cheer and provoke you to mirth;
Many feastings and frolics to add to your girth."

We wish you joy on your birthday
And all of the year through,
For all the best that life can hold
Is none too good for you.

To the birthday girl:
How am I to remember your birthday when you never look any
older?

To the most closely guarded secret in this country—your real age.

I raise my glass to say,
It's your Birthday, that's true;
And to celebrate the fact
That I'm younger than you.

To fine traditions like birthday spankings!

To a person who has matured so that she no longer shouts "Go
for it," but now calmly says "Have it delivered."

Although another year is past
You seem no older than the last!

Time marches on
Now tell the truth—
Where did you find
The fountain of youth?

To our favorite old hippie:
Let me assure you that this is a real celebration, and not an acid
flashback.

To middle age, which Don Marquis once described as, "the time when a man is always thinking that in a week or two he will feel as good as ever. "

In the words of Ben Jonson,
"To the old, long life and treasure;
To the young, all health and pleasure."

To middle age, when we begin to exchange our emotions for symptoms.

To our friend, who is aging wonderfully:
Nothing about you is old, except a few of your jokes.

Here's to a man who's discovered what really separates the men from the boys—many years.

To Europe, where they believe that women get more attractive after 35.

To age:
In the words of Frank Lloyd Wright, "The longer I live, the more beautiful life becomes."

Here's to absent friends—both the long-lost friends of our youth and our own long-lost youth.

May your fire never go out.
May your well never run dry.

May the Lord love us but not call us too soon.

May time never turn your head gray.

To wine:
It improves with age—I like it more the older I get.

"Old wood to burn, old wine to drink,
old friends to trust,
and old authors to read."
—Francis Bacon

May the clouds in your life be only a background for a lovely sunset.

In the words of Oliver Goldsmith, "I love everything that's old: old friends, old times, old manners, old books, old wine."

Here's a health to the future;
A sigh for the past;
We can love and remember,
And hope to the last,
And for all the base lies
That the almanacs hold
While there's love in the heart,
We can never grow old.

In the words of Larry E. Johnson,
"May our lives, like the leaves of the maple, grow
More beautiful as they fade.
May we say our farewells, when it's time to go,
All smiling and unafraid."

May you live to be a hundred—and decide the rest for yourself.

Here's to you:
May you live as long as you want to,
May you want to as long as you live.

To old age:
May it always be ten years older than I am.

To the "metallic" age—gold in our teeth, silver in our hair, and lead in our pants.

May the pleasures of youth never bring us pain in old age.

To old age, or, as William Allen White said on his 70th birthday, "I am not afraid of tomorrow, for I have seen yesterday and I love today."

To old age:
It's not how old you are, but how you are old.

To my old friend, as Marjorie Barstow Breenbie once said, "Beautiful young people are accidents of nature. But beautiful old people are works of art."

May you enter heaven late.

The good die young. Here's to hoping you live to a ripe old age.

May you live to be as old as your jokes.

To the old cronies:
May they never be too old to be young.

May we keep a little of the fuel of youth to warm our body in old age.

May we live to learn well,
And learn to live well.

May we never do worse.

May we never feel want, nor ever want feeling.

Bon Voyage Party

It's not just absence that makes the heart grow fonder, it's also the prospect of absence. As the time approaches when friends will go on an adventure, you naturally start thinking about how much you will miss them, even in the age of e-mail. This swelling emotion is best expressed in a toast.

As Kermit the Frog said, "Wherever you go, there you are."

As we say farewell,
Pleasure is mixed with pain,
Happy to meet, sorry to part,
Happy to meet again.

"A health to the man on the trail tonight;
may his grub hold out; may his dogs keep their legs; may his matches never misfire."
—Jack London

"I've traveled many a highway.
I've walked for many a mile.
Here's to the people who made my day—

To the people who waved and smiled."
—Tom T. Hall

To seasickness—traveling over the water by rail.

Here's to travel, which, as Benjamin Disraeli said, "teaches toleration."

To Kurt Vonnegut who said, "Unusual travel suggestions are dancing lessons from the gods."

As Mikey said in the Life cereal commercials,
"Try it. You'll like it."

Here's to you and here's to me,
Wherever we may roam;
And here's to the health and happiness
Of the ones who are left at home.

"Wealth I ask not, hope nor love,
Nor a friend to know me,
All I ask is the heav'n above,
And the roads below me!"
—Robert Louis Stevenson

Take a trail, good friend. And luck to you!

May bad fortune follow you all your days
And never catch up with you.

May the strength of three be in your journey.

Bris

A bris is the occasion on which a Jewish male infant is circumsized. It traditionally occurs on the eighth day after the child is born, and is a naming ceremony much like a Christian baptism. This is a good time for Best Wishes toasts as well (Chapter 5).

L'chayim (To Life)!

Mazel tov (Congratulations)!

Here's to our next generation.

Here's to our ancestors, who are smiling now.

To babies:
They will make love stronger, days shorter, nights longer, bankroll smaller, homes happier, clothes shabbier, the past forgotten, and the future worth living for.

To the new baby, who, as the parents will soon find out, is the perfect example of minority rule.

As they say in the diaper business, bottoms up.

Brunch

Brunches are scheduled for all sorts of reasons. One of the most common is to allow people to sleep late after a night of revelry. On those occasions, people often like to say a few words as they sip a bit of the "hair of the dog" that bit them the night before.

To strong, hot coffee:
It's what I'll take
Tomorrow morning
For my headache.

In the words of Lord Byron,
"Let us have wine and women, mirth and laughter,
Sermons and soda water the day after.

"Drink today and drown all sorrow;
You shall, perhaps, not do it tomorrow."
—Francis Beaumont & John Fletcher

To the hangover:
Something to occupy the head that wasn't used the night before.

To the irony of intoxication:
It makes you feel sophisticated, without being able to pronounce it.

Here's to the good time we must have had.

Here's hoping that no one had a camera last night.

In the words of Dr. Doran,
"See the wine in the bowl, how it sparkles tonight.
Tell us what can compete with that red sea of light
Which breathes forth a perfume that deadens all sorrow,
And leaves us blessed now, with a headache tomorrow."

First the man takes a drink;
Then the drink takes a drink,
Then the drink takes the man.

Why is it that my tongue grows loose
Only when I grow tight?

To William Temple who summed it up best when he said,
"The first glass for myself, the second for my friends;
The third for good humor, and the fourth for mine enemies."

A gilded mirror, a polished bar,
A million glasses, straws in a jar,
A courteous young man, all dressed in white,
Are my recollections of last night!
And with morning came bags of ice
So very necessary in this life of vice;
And when I cooled my throbbing brain,
Did I swear off and quit? No, I got soused again.

Building Dedication

When buildings are finished, there is often a ceremony to dedicate them. It's an occasion to thank the people who did the building, as well as the people who provided the funding. You may also want to look at the toasts listed in the Architects and Builders sections in Special People (Chapter 4).

To this wonderful building:
May it stand forever and a day.

To this building: A miracle of art and science.

To the architect:
Whose vision is now a reality.

To the roof and to the floor:
Now let's open up the door.

Business Dinner

Business dinners are most often the place for conservative toasts. If your hosts toast you, you toast them, and perhaps their company, back. No matter how friendly the occasion seems to be getting, it is still a business occasion. When in doubt, you can toast the glories of business itself. Avoid patriotic toasts at business occasions unless you know everyone in the room; businesses of all sizes are becoming global and a patriotic toast can inject the wrong note.

To the most important trend in business:
Not "e-commerce," but "we-commerce." Here's to us and our mutual prosperity.

To the good old days:
When big spenders used their own money!

Here's to our capital ideas!

To prosperity:
For, as John Ray said, "Money cures melancholy."
Here's to the most important people in the world:
Our customers.

May the weight of our taxes never bend the back of our credit.

In this world of depreciating assets, let's take a moment to appreciate our colleagues. Cheers to all of us!

To the almighty dollar:
Without it, we would have no cents.

To money:
The finest linguist in the world.

To the power of money:

As Clint W. Murchison said, "Money is like manure. If you spread it around, it does a lot of good, but if you pile it up in one place, it stinks like hell."

To all the pleasures that other people's money pays for.

To good will, which Marshall Field called, "the one and only asset that competition cannot undersell or destroy."

May we always be fired with enthusiasm for our work, and never fired enthusiastically by our clients.

Here's to our luck in working at a place where the principals have principles!

To the entrepreneur:
He knows money doesn't talk nowadays, it goes without saying.

To the company we keep profitable.

Christening
see Baptism/Christening (page 45)

Christmas

Christmastime is, as one song goes, a most wonderful time of the year. At the time of year when daylight is at its shortest, people get together and lighten things up with heartfelt toasts. In recent years, many hosts and guests have substituted the words "The Holidays" for "Christmas" so their toasts can be more inclusive and suitable for more people.

Here's to the holly with its bright red berry.
Here's to Christmas, let's make it merry.

I know I've wished you this before
But every year I wish it more.
A Merry Christmas.

Here's to St. Nick.

To Christmas:
Hang up love's mistletoe over the earth,
And let us kiss under it all the year round.

A Christmas wish:
May you never forget what is worth remembering or remember what is best forgotten.

Be merry all, be merry all,
With holly dress the festive hall,
Prepare the song, the feast, the ball,
To welcome Merry Christmas.

May peace and plenty be the first
To lift the latch on your door,
And happiness be guided to your home
By the candle of Christmas.

Now, thrice welcome, Christmas!
Which brings us good cheer,
Mince pies and plum pudding—
Strong ale and strong beer!

To a person so generous that it makes me want to say, "Yes, my friends, there is a Santa Claus."

In the immortal words of Tiny Tim in Charles Dicken's *A Christmas Carol*, "Here's to us all! God bless us every one!"

"Christmas...
A day when cheer and gladness blend,
When heart meets heart
And friend meets friend."
—J.H. Fairweather

I wish you a Merry Christmas
And a Happy New Year,
A pocket full of money
And a cooler full of beer.

May yours be the first house in the city to welcome St. Nicholas.

Here's to the red of the mistletoe,
And to its many leaves so green;

And here's to the lips of ruby red,
Waiting 'neath to complete the scene.

Here's to friends we've yet to meet,
Here's to those here; all here I greet;
Here's to childhood, youth, old age,
Here's to prophet, bard and sage,
Here's to your health may all be bright
On this so special Christmas night.

"At Christmas play and make good cheer
For Christmas comes but once a year."
—Thomas Turner

Here's wishing you more happiness
Than all my words can tell.
Not just alone for Christmas,
But for all the year as well.

Here's to holly and ivy hanging up,
And to something wet in every cup.

A Merry Christmas this December,
To a lot of folks I don't remember.

Then here's to the heartening wassail,
Wherever good fellows are found;
Be its master instead of its vassal,
And order the glasses around.
—Ogden Nash

Church Supper

Even at suppers in churches and synagogues where the congregation may not drink alcohol, there are toasts.

Where there is no vision, the people perish. *Proverbs* 29:18

The truth shall set you free. *John* 8:32

Eat thy bread with joy, and drink thy wine with a merry heart.
Ecclesiastes 9:7

Forsake not an old friend, for the new is not comparable to him. A new friend is as new wine: When it is old, thou shalt drink it with pleasure. *Ecclesiastes* 9:10

The best wine . . . that goeth down sweetly, causing the lips of those that are asleep to speak. *Song of Solomon* 7:9

Wine was created, from the beginning, to make men joyful, and not to make men drunk. Wine drunk with moderation is the joy of the soul and the heart. *Ecclesiastes* 31:35-36

To eat, to drink, and be merry. *Ecclesiastes* 8:15

Let us eat and drink: For tomorrow we shall die. *Isaiah* 22:13

A feast is made for laughter, and wine maketh merry. *Ecclesiastes* 10:19

Drink no longer water, but use a little wine for thy stomach's sake. *I Timothy* 5:23

Give...wine unto those that be of heavy hearts. *Proverbs* 31:6

Wine maketh glad the hearts of man. *Psalms* 104:15

Wine, which cheereth God and man. *Judges* 9:15

As we have therefore opportunity, let us do good unto all men. *Galatians* 6:10

Cinco de Mayo

May 5th is a great day to extend our compliments and our best wishes to the United States' neighbor to the south. Like Independence Day and Bastille Day, Cinco de Mayo is a revolutionary holiday best celebrated without getting into specific politics.

Salud (Health)!

Viva Mexico!

Here's to us drinking
A few more trays a
Delicious Cold
Cerveza

Here's to the agave blue
And the things its juice can do to you.

Here's to the fifth
It's almost gone.

Confirmation/First Communion

Confirmation and First Communion are Christian rites of passage in which a young person takes adult responsibility for their own faith. This is a happy moment, especially for the people who have been charged with the religious instruction of the confirmee. The godparents are now, officially, off duty. (Although some are lucky enough to have a godparent continue to watch over them long after Confirmation.) For this occasion, you might also want to consider some of the more sincere toasts in the Best Wishes (Chapter 5).

Here's to you, and here's to us! Know that confirmation does not mean that you are now on your own. It means that you are a full-fledged member in the family of God. Welcome. Here's to you!

Here's to you:
You have just taken the most important step you will ever take.

Welcome to the fellowship. We toast your calling.

To the parents and godparents who kept you safe and have started you on the right path.

Consolation Party

Everybody toasts when they have won; but it is probably even more important to toast when your team has lost. After all, it's not whether you win or lose, it's how you celebrate the outcome that matters.

To Ruth Gordon, who said "I think there is one smashing rule: Never face the facts."

Here's to doing better next year.

To the School of Hardknocks:
May we graduate from it someday.

"'Tis better to have loved and lost,
Than never to have loved at all."
—Lord Alfred Tennyson

Here's to revenge:
May we taste it some day!

Here's to the men who lose:
It is the vanquished's praises that I sing,
And this is the toast I choose:
"A hard-fought failure is a noble thing!
Here's to the men who lose."

To our defeat:
For, if experience is the best teacher, we are now truly educated.

Here's to the wisdom of the saying,
"If at first you don't succeed,
Adjust your goals."

To us:
Because any direction we go from here is up.

Let us continue with the resolve of the gladiators who turned to the stands as they entered the arena and said, "Those about to die salute you."

In the words of John F. Kennedy, "Our task is not now to fix blame for the past, but to fix the course for the future."

Here's to our opponents victory:
May they soon demonstrate that "what goes up, must come down."

You guys deserved to win. But as Ned Kelly, the Australian outlaw said while being hung, "Such is life."

You all worked hard on this campaign, and you should congratulate yourselves. To quote Beethoven's last words: "Friends applaud, the comedy is over."

Michel de Montaigne said, "There are some defeats more triumphant than victories." This was one of them. Here's to us.

Divorce

Divorce was once something that was spoken of in hushed tones. Today, with about half of all marriages ending in divorce, it's appropriate not only to speak of it, but occasionally even to toast it. After all, while many people get divorced, many of them go on to remarry. So, you can sometimes look at divorce not as an indictment of marriage, but as a desire to have one's marriage be all that it can be. Whether people are happy or sad to be divorced, getting divorced was probably an ordeal, so they deserve a toast.

'Tis better to have loved and lost
Than to marry and be bossed.

To Zsa Zsa Gabor who said, "I never hated a man enough to give him his diamond back."

Here's to the high rate of divorce which Morton Hunt said, "reflects not so much the failure of love as the determination of people not to live without it."

To alimony:
The high cost of loving.

To alimony:
Man's best proof that you have to pay for your mistakes.

To alimony:
Giving comfort to the enemy.

Here's to your divorce and the messy split:
We're all very happy you got rid of that shit.

To divorce:
The screwing you get for the screwing you got.

Easter

Easter is, for Christians, a joyous occasion. It is the day to celebrate the Resurrection, put on new bonnets, and enjoy the spring weather. An appropriate toast is a great way to share your Easter joy.

Through Adam, all died.
Through Christ, we all live.
May we live in his light.

To victory over death.

All rise and toast he who is risen from the dead.

Let us toast another mystery:
How they decide when Easter is each year!

May you be as bright and sunny
As the smiley Easter bunny.

Election Victory

An election victory is a very special moment. You have won, but you will probably need to work with the person you defeated at some point in your career.

Here's to democracy.

Here's to the wisdom of the public. May I be worthy of the honor they have given me.

To the team that got me here! This victory is yours.

To my opponent, for a hard fought battle.

To all the citizens,
Good and bad
And even that guy,
Dimpled Chad.

Family Reunion

Family reunions call for toasts. You can use one provided below, or you can look further in the Best Wishes (Chapter 5). You can also find good toasts for various family members in Special People (Chapter 4).

Here's to us that are here,
to you that are there,
and the rest of us everywhere.

Here's to your health, and your family's good health. May you live long and prosper.

To those who know me best and, for some reason, still love me.

May we be loved by those we love.

To the sap in our family tree.

Here's a toast to all who are here,
No matter where you're from;
May the best day you have ever seen
Be worse than the worst to come.

To our differences,
To common ground,
To what we're seeking,
To what we've found,
To what brings us together,
To what sets us apart,
To many different folks
United with one heart.

To the good old days:
When we weren't so good, because we weren't so old.

Your health! May we drink one together in ten years time and a few in between.

Farewell

There are may reasons for a farewell toast. Some are made as people leave on trips (see the Bon Voyage toasts section in this chapter.) Others are made at the end of an evening. The most bittersweet ones are made when you don't know whether you will see the person again. Many people prefer to say "farewell," which they feel is temporary, instead of "goodbye," which they feel could be permanent. If, however, the person you are toasting is no longer alive, you may want to look at the Memorial/ Funeral Gathering toasts in this chapter. You can also turn almost any of the Best Wishes toasts into a farewell toast just by adding the words "Farewell for now."

May you sleep like a log, but not like a sawmill.

To all, to each, a fair good-night,
And pleasant dreams and slumbers light.
—Sir Walter Scott

Good day, good health, good cheer, good night!
To goodbyes—that they never be spoken.
To friendships—may they never be broken.

May we always part with regret and meet again with pleasure.

"The pain of parting," said Charles Dickens, "is nothing to the joy of meeting again."

Good-bye, dear ones, and if you need a friend,
How happy I will be,
Should you get tired of life's rough way
Just come and lean on me.
I'll take you on the smoothest road that God to man e'er gave;
And will go by the longest way that takes us to the grave.

In the words of *Star Trek*'s Mr. Spock, "Live long and prosper."

May your fire never go out.

May your well never run dry.

May the Lord love us, but not call us too soon.

May you live to be a hundred years with one extra year to repent.

Long life to you and may you die in your bed.

May your enemies never meet a friend.

May the saints protect you, and sorrow neglect you, and bad luck to the one that doesn't respect you.

May you live to be a hundred—and decide the rest for yourself.

May time never turn your head gray.

"Were't the last drop in the well,
As I gasp'd upon the brink,
Ere my fainting spirit fell,
'Tis to thee that I would drink."
—Lord Byron

May we never grumble without cause,
And may we never have cause to grumble.

May we live respected and die regretted.

May your voyage through life be as happy and as free
As the dancing waves on the deep blue sea.

May you be hung, drawn, and quartered:
Hung in the hall of fame,
Drawn by a golden chariot,
And quartered in the arms of the one you love best.

May we each offer love to one, friendship to many, and good will to all.

May the most you wish for be the least you get.

As you slide down the bannister of life
May the splinters never face the wrong way.

Here's to turkey when you're hungry,
Champagne when you are dry,
A pretty girl when you need her,
And heaven when you die.

May the road rise to meet you.
May the wind be always at your back,
the sun shine warm upon your face,
the rain fall soft upon your fields,
and until we meet again
may God hold you in the hollow of His hand.

May each of us be what he or she wants to be.

All the best to you, from one who remembers when you were an immature brat...last week.

To quote from the immortal bard Shakespeare's *Henry VIII*, "A health, gentlemen, Let it go 'round."

As Shakespeare said in *The Merchant of Venice*, "I wish you all the joy you can wish."

May bad fortune follow you all of your days—and never catch up with you!

May poverty always be a day's march behind us.

I wish you all the best. As Shakespeare said in *Timon of Athens*, May "The best of happiness, honor and fortunes keep with you."

When we are right, may it be long remembered.
When we are wrong, may it be soon forgotten.

May we never speak to deceive nor listen to betray.

May we never know want until relief is at hand.

May you die in bed at age ninety-five shot by the jealous husband of a teenage wife.

May you enter Heaven late.

May the saints protect you,
And sorrow neglect you,
And bad luck to the one
That doesn't respect you.

Father's Day

To Dad:
Even though you never get our names right, we know you love
us.

To the new father:
Good luck as you enter a "changing" world.

To Dad:
You gave us life,
You gave us your name,
So for all of our faults,
We think you're to blame.

To Dad:
It's marvelous to see how you keep maturing.

To Dad:
I'll never be able to fill your shoes. In fact, I can't stand to get
within ten feet of them.

To Dad:
May the love and respect we express toward him make up for the
worry and care we have visited upon him.

To Dad:
You raised me, so I raise a glass to you.

To my father:
If I can become half the man he is, I'll have achieved greatness.

First Communion
see Confirmation/First Communion (page 63)

Fishing Party

People who fish love to talk about fishing. So, of course, they are natural toasters. Often they have a good sense of humor, so you can use toasts that have hook, as well as those that have allure. You can toast someone for being great at casting or skilled at tying flies.

To sending flies flying and starting fish frying.

Here's to our fisherman bold;
Here's to the fish he caught;
Here's to the one that got away,
And here's to the ones he bought.

To things that swim and have scales,
And are smaller than whales.

A fisherman, between you and I
Will very seldom tell a lie—
Except when it is needed to
Describe the fish that left his view.

Here's to filling your creel
With a tasty meal.

As Don Marquis once said, "Here's to Fishing—a grand delusion enthusiastically promoted by glorious liars in old clothes."

We fall for his tales
Hook, line, and sinker,
He doesn't catch much,
But he's a great thinker.

Here's to the fish that I may catch:
So large that even I,
When talking of it afterward,
Will never need to lie.

Here's to the great fisherman:
Sometimes you meet people and there's just something about them that tells you this is a person who fishes. I think it's the smell.

May the holes in your net be no bigger than your fish.

May your line never snap,
May you never jam your reel,
May your pole never start
To bend like an eel!

Here's to rod and line:
May they never part company.

Most people zip flies. Here's to the guys who tie them.

Here's to our favorite fisherman:
May he live to see his stories come true.

Here's to the one that got away!

Here's to the folks who know that old fishers
never die—they just smell that way.

Here's to the noble sport of fishing:
A hobby that we are all hooked on!

Let's lift our glass to the creative fisherman:
Every time he talks about the one that got away,
it grows another foot.

May good things come to those who bait.

Football/Soccer Event

We don't recommend toasting while playing football. However, fans will find ample opportunity for toasting before games, while watching them, at the start of the season, at the end of the season, between seasons, and a few times in-between.

Here's to the pigskin:
As Frank Gifford said, "Football is like nuclear warfare. There are no winners, only survivors."

Here's to people who have goals!

To learning to play through pain:
As Vince Lombardi said, "Nobody is hurt. Hurt is in the mind. If you can walk, you can run."

Here's to Football;
It's not merely a contact sport. It's a collision sport.

To the gridiron:
May we never commit offenses on defense, and may we never be defensive about our offense.

Here's to your courage:
May you be strong,
Especially when it's
Third and long.

Fourth of July

You will also find many suitable toasts for this occasion in Patriotic Toasting (Chapter 8).

May we always remember the words of Epicetus who said, "Only the educated are free."

My country, great and free!
Heart of the world, I drink to thee!

May we be slaves to no party and bigots to no sect.

As Byron said, "He who loves not his country can love nothing."

Here's to the memory
Of the man
That raised the corn
That fed the goose

That bore the quill
That made the pen
That wrote the Declaration of Independence.

In the immortal words of Daniel Webster,
"It is my loving sentiment, and by the blessing of God it shall be my dying sentiment—Independence now and Independence forever!"

To the Fourth of July:
For like chowder, it cannot be enjoyed without crackers.

Here's to our country's birthday.

Fraternal Event

Fraternities often have their own elaborate toasting rituals. For example, a Web site from a Masonic organization specifies, "the Officers and Brethren will retire to the banquet room for what is often referred to as the Festive Board. This gathering is opened with grace, conducted with certain toasts, and closed with the Tyler's Toast."

Some fraternal toasts are carefully worded or even secret. In some cases, only particular members or officers are supposed to know and participate in certain toasts. When you join a new organization, learning the appropriate toasts is a good first step.

Here's to you and here's to me,
Wherever we may roam;
And here's to the health and happiness
Of the ones who are left at home.

"The Fraternity of Man—God born and God blessed—its mighty influence for man's betterment can be measured by no human means."
—Frederick W. Craig

As we say farewell,
Pleasure is mixed with pain,
Happy to meet, sorry to part,
Happy to meet again.

As we meet on the level, may we part on the square.

In the words of Thomas Carlyle, "A mystic bond of brotherhood makes all men one." Here's to my brothers.

Friends Dinner

Whenever friends gather, toasts are in order. You can also find toasts about friends in Special People (Chapter 4).

There are good ships, and there are wood ships,
The ships that sail the sea.
But the best ships, are friendships,
And may they always be.

May the roof above us never fall in.
And may the friends gathered below it never fall out.

Forsake not an old friend, for the new is not comparable to him.

A new friend is as new wine:
When it is old, thou shalt drink it with pleasure.

Always remember to forget
The friends that proved untrue.
But never forget to remember
Those that have stuck by you.

'Tis better to buy a small bouquet
And give to your friend this very day,
Than a bushel of roses white and red
To lay on his coffin after he's dead.

Who is a friend but someone to toast,
Someone to gibe, someone to roast.
My friends are the best friends
Loyal, willing, and able.
Now let's get to drinking!
Glasses off the table!

Friendship's the wine of life.
Let's drink of it and to it.

My heart is as full as my glass when I drink to you, old friend.

Fundraising

There are many approaches to fundraising. One is to pester people and wear them down. Another is to make them feel guilty. But, undoubtedly, the best and most enjoyable approach is to create situations where you can thank your donors and your fundraisers with a cheery toast. You may also want to consider the toasts listed under Benefactors in Special People (Chapter 4).

As Francis Bacon said, "In charity there is no excess."

To the best of all nations: Donation.

To a person so generous that it makes me want to say, "Yes, my friends, there is a Santa Claus."

As we have therefore opportunity, let us do good unto all men. *Galatians* 6:10

May the heart that melts at the sight of sorrow always be blessed with the means to relieve it.

Here's riches to the generous and power to the merciful.

May we strengthen the weak,
Give light to the blind,
Clothe the naked,
And be friends to mankind.

Here's to those of us who work for charity:
We have to, nobody will pay us.

To charity:
Unless a man is a recipient of charity, he should be a contributor to it.

In the words of Alexander Pope,
"In faith and hope the world will disagree,
But all mankind's concern is charity."

To our benefactor, a person who, in the words of Chauncey Depew, "makes two smiles grow where one grew before."

The best way I can think of to ask for your support is to use the words that the famous suffragette Lucy Stone chose for her last words, "Make the world better".

In the words of Josh Billings, "Remember the poor—it costs nothing."

To the spirit of charity:
As Clint W. Murchison said, "Money is like manure. If you spread it around, it does a lot of good, but if you pile it up in one place, it stinks like hell."

Funeral
see Memorial/Funeral Gathering **below**

Gambling Party

Back when gambling was frowned upon by many in society, those who gambled often liked to drink and toast. Today, in part because of state-sponsored lotteries and office pools, gambling seems to be more widely accepted. People regularly discuss the odds on sporting events. Schools and charities even host "Casino" fund-raising events. And, of course, people still like to toast both their good and bad fortunes.

A little whiskey now and then
Is relished by the best of men;
It surely drives away dull care,
And makes ace high look like two pair.

When you win a fortune, may you remember your friends.

As the song goes, "Luck be a lady tonight."

Here's to poker:
It's like a glass of beer—you draw to fill.

Here's to Lady Luck:
May she never desert us.

The hand that rocks the cradle
Is the hand that rules the earth.
But the hand that holds four aces—
Bet on it all you're worth!

May your women be stacked, and not your deck.

Life consists not in holding good cards, but in playing those you hold well.

To the race track
Where windows clean people.

Golf Party

When you get to the 19th hole and it's time for toasting, you should still maintain your form. Keep your head up, don't lose your grip, and follow through.

Let's lift our glasses. And if we spill a drop, let's take a mulligan!

To golf, the most frustrating and masochistic sport in the world. That may be why golf spelled backwards is flog.

May you learn to drive the golf ball as well as you drive the golf cart.

Here's to the golfer who just missed a hole-in-one by three strokes.

To our favorite golfer:
May he always be able to find his balls.

May his investments always be above par, and his game always below.

May your putter never fail you.

Grace

Grace isn't necessarily a toast. Many who make it a habit to say grace before a meal prefer to clasp hands rather than clasp glasses. However, the comments that people use as graces almost always make excellent toasts.

In the words of the cowboys, "Bless this food and us that eats it."

Heavenly father bless us,
And keep us all alive;
There's ten of us for dinner
And not enough for five.

For what we are about to receive, may the Lord make us truly thankful.

To this meal:
In the words of Anthelme Brillat-Savarin, here's to "The creator forcing man to take in food for living invites him through appetite and rewards him with pleasure."

Good food,
Good meat,
Good God,
Let's eat!

For every cup and plateful,
God make us truly grateful

God is great and God is good,
And we thank him for our food.
By his hand we all are fed;
Give us Lord, our daily bread.

Thank You for the world so sweet,
Thank You for the food we eat,
Thank You for birds that sing,
Thank You God, for everything.
—E. Rutter Leatham

Rub-a-dub-dub.
Thanks for the grub.
Yeah, God!

Graduation

Graduations are wonderful moments. Everyone is happy—both the student who has made it through the particular program or course of study, and all those who supported the student, in one way or another, through the journey. Clearly, it's time for a toast.

To the future and the leaders of tomorrow.

Let him be kept from paper, pen, and ink.
That he may cease to write and learn to think.

A toast to the Graduate:
She's in a class by herself.

I don't want to waste my chance to give you good advice as you go out into the world, so I'll use the words that the famous suffragette, Lucy Stone, chose for her last words, "Make the world better".

Pete Seeger said that, "Education is when you read the fine print; experience is what you get when you don't." You've got the education, so you should be able to skip some of the experience. Good Luck.

To all who have just graduated:
May you now go on to become educated.

To our fine educations:
May they go to our heads!

Jacob Bronowski said, "It is important that students bring a certain ragamuffin, barefoot irreverence to their studies; they are not here to worship what is known, but to question it." Here's to hoping that what we have learned will keep us questioning.

William Hazlitt said that, "Learning is its own exceeding great reward." So don't expect good jobs! But here's to school anyway.

Epicetus said, "Only the educated are free." I say, only the graduated are free. Here's to our freedom!

Gaudeamus igitur
Iuvenes dum sumus.
Post iucundum iuventutes
Post molestam senectutem
Nos habebit humus.
If Mr. Blair, our long-suffering Latin teacher who put up with our jokes and ad libs, such as "Ding, Dingere, Dong, Dongus" will pardon the translation, this toast means, more or less,
Let us rejoice,
While we are young.
After happy youth,
After annoying old age,
We will end up in the ground.

Homecoming

If you toast someone's departure at a bon voyage party, it only makes sense to toast their return, as well. If you are looking for toasts for a college homecoming weekend, look under Football or Victory Celebration (pgs. 74 and 116).

Let us remember home while we are here, and all those we meet here when we return home.

John F. Kennedy's father, Joseph P. Kennedy, said "He may be President, but he still comes home and swipes my socks."
Welcome home. We're happy to stock up.

To you:
This will always be your home—where you'll always find warm words on a cold day.

Home has been called the place where we receive the best treatment and which we appreciate the least. Despite your griping, we love you. Cheers!

Here's to home where a world of strife is shut out and a world of love is shut in. And to you being here.

Welcome back to where you belong.

Housewarming

Even if the people holding the housewarming have been in the house for two years redecorating, it is still worth holding a housewarming. If you like the people, bring along a bottle or two to help them stock their refreshments supply, and start the toasting.

Here's to your cozy hearth.

May your home be warmed by the love of family and friends.

Thank you for turning this wonderful house into a home.

May your fire be as warm as the weather is cold.

Welcome neighbor.
Know that tomorrow
I will be back here
Asking to borrow.
Cheers!

May your well never run dry.

To home:
Where we always find warm words on a cold day.

To home:
The place where we receive the best treatment and which we appreciate the least.

Here's to home where a world of strife is shut out and a world of love is shut in.

God bless this mess.

God bless our mortgaged home.

Here's to our town:
A place where people spend money they haven't earned to buy things they don't need to impress people they don't like.

"The ornament of a house is the guests who frequent it."
—Ralph Waldo Emerson

To the pleasures of home: a good book, a bright light, and an easy chair.

To home:
The place where you're treated best and grumble most.

To home:
The father's kingdom, the child's paradise, and the mother's world.

As the old song says:
"On my!
I'm too young to die!
I wanna go home!"

Hunting Party

Hunting, feasting, and toasting go together, but it's best if the toasting starts after the shooting is all over. If it's a rowdy hunting party, you can use toasts from the Bachelor Party section of Words for Weddings (Chapter 2).

Here's to our game, and here's to our aim.

To the chase and to the kill!

May we shoot straight and never late.

International Meeting

Today, almost every business is global. When people from different countries and cultures socialize, the best common language is often a toast. If you're the host, make the first toast to your guests or to your joint venture. After that, use a toast like the ones here that celebrate international business.

As they say at Disney, it's a small world after all.

Here's to Marshall McLuhan's thought that we all live in the same global village.

Here's to Spaceship Earth, and all our fellow astronauts.

Here's to the common culture of the world: Commerce.

I have learned that we are all very different, and, as the French say, Vive La Difference!

Kwanza

Kwanza is an African-American festival that is celebrated near the end of the year. While it is close to Christmas on the calendar, it is closer to Thanksgiving in spirit because it is based on harvest celebrations. At the Kwanza ceremonies I have attended, specific African words are used on specific days in rituals, but I have never heard them used as toasts. The toasts given are in English, but evidently follow the same themes as the words in the rituals.

To our people!

Let's drink to our heritage.

To unity:
May we always be one.

May we always be our own masters.

Launch

Nobody *starts* anything anymore. People *launch* everything from products to programs and from coalitions to campaigns. One of the reasons you have an official launch is to get everyone working happily together. Here are a few words that may be right.

Here's to us and to our mission.

May your business be like the capital of Ireland:
Always Dublin!

Ten, nine, eight, seven, six, five, four, three, two, one. Lift off your glasses, we're in business.

Ten, nine, eight, seven, six, five, four, three, two, one...and may that be the last thing that this team does backwards!

To the power of the human spirit:
In the words of William Faulkner, "I believe that man will not merely endure, he will prevail...because he has a soul, a spirit capable of compassion and sacrifice and endurance."

To quote Victor Hugo, "If we must suffer, let us suffer nobly."

To quote the Nike ad campaign, "Just Do It."

May we be judged by our actions. As Shakespeare said, "Action is eloquence."

I don't want to waste my chance to give a toast, so I'll use the words that the famous suffragette Lucy Stone chose for her last words, "Make the world better".

May we be like mighty oaks, which, after all, are only acorns that held their ground.

Let us go forth with the resolve of the gladiators who turned to the stands as they entered the arena and said, "Those about to die salute you."

Anthropologist Margaret Mead said, "Never doubt that a small group of thoughtful, committed citizens can change the world. Indeed, it's the only thing that ever has." And since we are committed, I believe that we can change the world. Let's do it! Cheers!

As we work together, may we follow the advice of Winston Churchill who said, "Never, never, never give up."

Let us remember the words of coach Vince Lombardi who said, "There's only one way to succeed in anything, and that is to give it everything." Cheers!

Library Dedication

Libraries are one of our greatest cultural institutions. (Of course, since I write for a living, I may be biased.) These treasure chests must be celebrated.

Here's to all these nooks for books.

Here's to our fine new library:
It speaks volumes about our community.

Cicero said "to add a library to a house is to give that house a soul." It follows that to give school a library is to give that school a soul. To our new library—the new soul of our school.

Here's to this library:

Praise for the people who run it is overdue. And so are most of the books.

To our library:
As Mrs. Lyndon Baines Johnson said, "Perhaps no place in any community is so democratic as the town library. The only entrance requirement is interest."

Memorial/Funeral Gathering

The sad fact is that most of us will have lots of opportunities to toast those who are no longer with us. While some people might want to be remembered with solemn sentences, most of the people I have talked to (and this may tell you something about my friends) say that after they have shuffled off, they would like to be remembered with a happy thought and a raised glass. There is something sweet and appropriate about remembering someone in the same way, and perhaps in the same place, in which you spent good times together.

To our dear departed:
As they say in postcards, wish you were here.

To live in hearts we leave behind is not to die.

To our dear departed:
That the devil mightn't hear of his death, 'till he's safe inside the walls of heaven.

To our dear departed friend:
Oliver Herford was right, "Only the good die young."

We cannot share this sorrow
If we haven't grieved a while.
But let us remember the best of our friend
'Cause that should make us smile.

I drink as the fates ordain it.
Come fill it and have done with rhymes.
Fill up the lovely glass and then drain it
In memory of dear old times.
—William Makepeace Thackeray

As Ralph Waldo Emerson suggested, "Let us make our glasses kiss; Let us quench the sorrow-cinders."

May every hair on her head turn into a candle to light the way to heaven, and may God and the Holy Mother take the harm of the years away from her.

"Oh, here's to other meetings,
And merry greetings then;
And here's to those we've drunk with.
But never can again."
—Stephen Decatur

Time cuts down all,
Both great and small.

"Now let's sit and drink and make us merry,
And afterward we will his body bury."
—Geoffrey Chaucer

Here's to the tears of affection,
May they crystallize as they fall,
And become pearls, that in the after years,
We'll wear in memory of those whom we have loved.

To our loved ones who have passed away:
May the winds of heaven whisper hourly benedictions over their
hallowed graves.

Let us remember the imortal words of Alfred, Lord Tennyson,
"I hold it true, whate'er befall,
I feel it when I sorrow most;
'Tis better to have loved and lost,
Than never to have loved at all."
We loved you. Here's to you!

*This is a long toast that I wrote for the people at a memorial gathering for
a friend that we could not attend in England. Feel free to adopt any or all of
it if you had the luck to know anybody who had this kind of spirit.*

"One of the least logical sources for a quote about Maria is the
musical *The Sound of Music*. But that work did ask the questions,
asked by so many employers and others during her life: 'How do
you solve a problem like Maria? How do you hold a rainbow in
your hand?' And that is, ultimately, an appropriate
question...because Maria was, in essence, light. Perhaps not
always a ray of hope, but always a hope of Ray. And it's deeper
than that.

"Like light, her properties were as fluid as a wave in some
interactions, and as hard-hitting as a particle in others.

"Gently warm at times, but incisive when focused and coherent.

"Capable of illuminating beauty as well as scorching that which
was rotten.

"When you got to know her, like light, she was made of a riot of
colors and shades and wavelengths. Light, as telecom veterans
know, when stimulated and decoded in the right ways, can carry
an amazing number of diverse messages, in both directions,
simultaneously, instantly, around the world.

"We all knew, better than she did, that Maria was like light—
fundamentally bright. A brightness measured in *whats:*
What were you thinking?

What are you feeling?
What about this?
What if?

"There's no need now to rage against the dying of this light. Light affects us for a long time after its fused. We'll be discovering energy reserves, and experiencing sun spots, for a while yet.

"How do you solve a problem like Maria? If she were here in a more physical way, she might ask if we were working on the right problem. And if she could have disassociated from herself, a process she would have had fun with, she would ask if things needed to be solved at all.

"Maria is now a part of our experience. And she would tell us to process that experience. Having been brightened, warmed, and occasionally tanned and burned by Maria was not an annunciation. No virgins here. But it was an illumination that calls for reflection.

"And if any one of us tried to bury what we felt about her, rather than feeling it, she would tell us, tersely, to remove the earth and grass we had piled on those feelings. She would command, Sod Off!"

Military Meals & Maneuvers

Here's to American valor:
May no war require it, but may it ever be ready for every foe.

In the words of Minna Thomas Antrim,
"Here's to Uncle Sam's fighters:
Models of all that's brave,
Terrors to all who are unfair."

Here's to the Army and Navy,
And the battles they have won.
Here's to America's colors—
The colors that never run.

Here's to the land we love and the love we land.

"The girl and boy are bound by a kiss,
But there's never a bond, old friend like this:
We have drunk from the same canteen."
—Gen. Charles G. Halpine

Here's to the soldier and his arms,
Fall in, men, fall in;
Here's to woman and her arms,
Fall in, men, fall in.

Air Force

Here's to our air cover!

They've got wings, but they're not always angels. Here's to our Air Force.

Here's to the ultimate jet set.

Army

Here's to the soldier who fights and loves:
May he never lack for either.

Here's to the bravest sons of guns!

The following toast has been called "The Ladies' Toast."
The soldiers of America,
Their arms our defense,
Our arms their recompense—
Fall in, men; fall in!

Marines

Here's health to you and to our corps,
Which we are proud to serve:
In many a strife we have fought for life
And never lost our nerve.
If the Army and the Navy
Ever look on heaven's scenes,
They will find the streets are guarded
By the United States Marines.

I give you muscles of steel, nerves of iron, tongues of silver, hearts of gold, necks of leather—the Marines.

As Sir Walter Scott said, "Tell that to the marines."

Navy

To the wisdom of sailors:
As Sir Walter Scott said, "Tell that to the marines—the sailors won't believe it."

To the wind that blows, the ship that goes, and the lass that loves a sailor.

In the words of Colonel Blacker, "Put your trust in God, boys, and keep your powder dry."

To our sailors:
Long may they ride the waves.

To our Navy:
May it ever float.

Here's to the ships of our navy,
And to the ladies of our land;
May the former be well rigged,
And the latter be well manned.

A stout ship, a clear sea, and a far-off coast in stormy weather.

Here's to foes well tarred and tars well feathered.

Here's to the Navy:
True hearts and sound bottoms.

Here's to grog, grub, and glory.

To the sailor:
The only person I know who gets seasick taking a bath.

Mother's Day

You will find other toasts about mothers listed under Mothers in Special People (Chapter 4).

Here's to a Mom so great that she makes
you understand why Mom upside down is Wow!

William Ross Wallace said, "The hand that rocks the cradle is the hand that rules the world." Here's to our mothers!

Mark Twain said "My mother had a great deal of trouble with me, but I think she enjoyed it." I say the same, and I apologize for all the trouble.

Rose Kennedy was a great mother. She summed up her philosophy and motivation by saying, "I looked on child-rearing not only as a work of love and duty but as a profession that was fully as interesting and challenging as any honorable profession in the world and one that demanded the best that I could bring it." Here's to mothers everywhere.

Pope Paul VI observed that "Every mother is like Moses. She does not enter the promised land. She prepares a world she will not see." Here's to that great sacrifice.

Ralph Waldo Emerson said,"Men are what their mothers made them." So I guess Dad gave me the name, but you get the blame. I love you, Mom.

Here's to Dr. Benjamin Spock who is one of the rare men to admit, "I really learned it all from mothers." You know, we all did. Cheers.

Movie Opening or Wrap
see Theater/Movie Opening or Wrap (page 113).

Music Recital

Music and toasting are natural companions. It's best, however, to wait until after a performance to propose a toast.

Here's to our star of note!

Here's to music:
Henry Wadsworth Longfellow called it "the universal language of mankind."

Here's to the performer:
She's better than me;
I could never
Stay on key!

To the soothing influence of music:
As William Congreve said, "Music hath charms to soothe the savage breast."

Here, here!
You pleased my ear!

To music, which John Erskine called, "the only language in which you cannot say a mean or sarcastic thing."

I never thought
I'd hear such a thing!
The sweet music shows
You've been practicing.

To music:
As Friedrich Nietzsche said, "Without music, life would be a mistake."

To mirth, music, and moderation:
Mirth at every board,
Music in all instruments,
Moderation in our desires.

Let's lift our glass to the conductor—a person who rarely composes himself.

New Neighbors

You may also find appropriate toasts listed earlier in this chapter under Housewarming (page 83).

May the main purpose of the fences between our homes be to support us while we gossip!

Here's to the views we share!

Robert Frost wrote that "Good fences make good neighbors." But don't feel that you have to worry about curtains. Cheers!

To the fences that separate us and the concerns that unite us.

To those we borrow from.

Here's to you:
And I say that knowing all about you. Remember the old saying: 'You can fool everyone except your neighbors.'

Here's to our new neighbors:
It's clear that you know what Franklin P. Jones said: "Nothing makes you more tolerant of a neighbor's party than being there."

John Donne said "No man is an island," And I say, "Don't be a stranger." Here's to a long friendship.

New Job

You can also use almost any Best Wishes toast when congratulating someone who has just been promoted.

Here's to the recognition of excellence.

Here's to all you've learned and the great new title that you have earned.

As you climb the ladder,
Rung by rung,
May you never slip,
And fall in dung!

New Year's Eve or New Year's Day

Try and get your toasting in before midnight on New Year's Eve. If you wait until midnight, you may not be able to be heard over all the carousing.

May we be alive at the same time next year!

May all our troubles in the coming year be as short-lived as our New Year's resolutions.

In the year ahead may we treat our friends with kindness and our enemies with generosity.

Here's to the magic of bubbling wine
And an evening with friends so true.
There's none I'd rather enjoy them with
Than you, and you, and you.

Welcome be ye that are here,
Welcome all, and make good cheer,
Welcome all, another year.

Another year is dawning. Let it be true
For better or for worse, another year with you.

Here's to a bright New Year
And a fond farewell to the old;
Here's to the things that are yet to come
And to the memories that we hold.

[After midnight]
One swallow doesn't make a summer, but it breaks a New Year's resolution. Cheers!

Ordination

My sister is an Episcopal minister, which means that she was ordained. (Not foreordained or preordained, that's another sect, evidently.) Most of the toasts at ordinations tend to be serious and scriptural. (These folks are accustomed to talking while raising chalices.) I didn't make it to her ceremony but, if I had, I might have been tempted to propose one of the following toasts:

Here's to the new minister:
May she learn
To give a sermon
That won't set
The congregation squirmin'.

To the new minister. Remember the rule:
I'll listen quietly,
If I'm in a pew,
But when I'm home.
I'll talk back to you.

Here's to the new minister:
Go follow your calling,
Without any stalling.

Passover

On Passover, a Jewish holy day, there is a traditional meal, called a Seder. There is a ritual text for the dinner and special foods. I have been to several Seders where toasting broke out after the ceremony.

Hag samayah. (Happy Holiday.)

To Elijah.

L'chayim (To Life)!

Mazel tov (Congratulations)!

Peace Party

You can toast peace as easily as you can toast war. You can also use toasting to make peace—drinking toasts with a former enemy can be like smoking a peace pipe. Some people liken toasting to shaking hands since in both cases you show that your dominant hand is not wielding a weapon.

As Shakespeare said in *The Merry Wives of Windsor*, let us "Drink down all unkindness"

May we love peace enough to fight for it.

May we love peace enough not to fight for it.

Here's to the proverbial soft answer
which turneth away wrath.

May our leaders be wise, and our commerce increase,
And may we experience the blessings of peace.

To peace! In the words of a great general, Dwight David
Eisenhower, "We know that there is no true and lasting cure for
world tensions in guns and bombs. We know that only in the
spirit and mind of men, dedicated to justice, and right, can, in
the long term, enable us to live in the confident tranquility that
should be every man's heritage."

Here's to health, peace, and prosperity:
May the flower of love never be nipped by the frost of
disappointment, nor the shadow of grief fall among a member of
this circle.

Here's to the blessings of the year,
Here's to the friends we hold so dear,
And to peace on earth, both far and near.

Political Parties

You only get to vote for each candidate once in each election, but
you can toast them as often as you wish.

Here's to our candidate! Let's vote with our glasses.

To Washington, our country's capital, where the roads, and
everything else, go around in circles.

Here's to the honest politician who, as defined by Simon
Cameron, "when he is bought, will stay bought."

Here's to the politician:
A person who straddles an issue when he isn't dodging one.

To the politician:
A person who divides his time between running for office and
running for cover.

Here's to our politician:
A man who stands for what he thinks others will fall for.

To our newly elected officials:
May they do only a minimal amount of damage this session.

To our flag. Long may it wave.
And to our politicians, long may they rave!

Give us pure candidates and a pure ballot box,
And our freedom shall stand as firm as the rocks.

Project Completion
see also Team Rally, Victory, **and** Consolation Party

Let's have a drink,
Let's have some fun
Because at last
The job is done.

Anthropologist, Margaret Mead, said, "Never doubt that a small group of thoughtful, committed citizens can change the world. Indeed, it's the only thing that ever has." And you have proved her right. Here's to you!

Here's to future generations:
They will be able to see farther because they will stand on the foundation that you have built. Cheers.

Promotion
see New Job (page 95).

Protest Meeting
Protesting is as American as the Boston Tea Party. We are a nation founded on protesting and righteous objection. If you're planning to speak out about something, be proud and toast your cause.

To the spirit of the Boston Tea Party.

To truth, not power.

To history:
She will vindicate us.

Mahatma Gandhi was right when he said, "Truth never damages a cause that is just." Here's to our just cause!

Barry H. Goldwater said "moderation in the pursuit of justice is no virtue." We are out for justice; let's go all the way. To victory!

To protest! May we never fail to rise up when the government falls down.

Davy Crockett's policy was "Be always sure you're right—then go ahead!" Well, we're right. So here's to what we are going to do.

Here's to those who have had the courage to speak out: They alone have served truth. As Henri Frederic Amiel said, "Truth is not only violated by falsehood; it may be equally outraged by silence."

Recovery
see Teetotalers Party (page 111).

Retirement

Despite the economy, some people still get to retire. That's worth toasting, because someday you may get to retire, too.

There's an old saying that describes a good life as
"Twenty years a child;
Twenty years running wild;
Twenty years a mature man,
and after that, praying."
You can probably skip the praying part. Not because you have been so good, but because you never went through the mature stage! All our best to you.

As they say in Ireland, "May you enjoy your new life."

To a man who now has the freedom to do all the things he spent the last 40 years dreaming of doing!

To our former colleague:
We don't know what we'll do without him...but we're sure eager to find out!

To your retirement:
A deserved reward for a job well done.

Here's to the holidays—all 365 of them.

Reunions

At any type of reunion, you can also use many of the Best Wishes Toasts (Chapter 5).

Merry met, and merry part,
I drink to thee with all my heart.

We gather today
To see those we have missed.
Especially the people
That we might have kissed.

Here's a toast to all who are here,
No matter where you're from:
May the best day you have ever seen
Be worse than the worst to come.

To the good old days:
When we weren't so good, because we weren't so old.

Your health. May we drink one together in ten years time and a few in between.

Here's to us that are here, to you that are there, and the rest of us everywhere.

To friends: As long as we are able
To lift our glasses from the table.

"But fill me with the old familiar juice,
Methinks I might recover bye and bye."
—Omar Khayyam

In the immortal words of William Makepeace Thackeray,
"I drink it as the fates ordain it,
Come, fill it, and have done with rhymes;
Fill up the lonely glass, and drain it
In memory of dear old times."

To the good old days, which we are having right now.

When we are gathered to carouse, there's a song that runs
through my head,
"Hail, hail, the gangs all here,
So what the hell do we care?
What the hell do we care?
Hail, hail, the gang's all here,
So what the hell do we care now?"

Roast

A roast is an event where all of the toasts, speeches, and jokes
insult the guest of honor. It may sound like a torture session, but people
with certain senses of humor love them, especially when the roastee is
witty and capable of giving as good as he or she gets. The harshness of
the insults show how close the roaster and the roastee are. The closer
your relationship to the roastee, the tougher you can be. If you really
know the person, they'll know that you still love them, no matter what
you are saying. There are, of course, certain exceptions. Don't talk
about someone's mother. For the record, its considered very bad form
to repeat anything you say or hear in a roast outside of the roast.

Here's to our guest of honor:
No matter what we do, we can't make an ass out of him. Nature
did that long ago.

To the woman of the hour:
There are many things I could say about her. That she's modest,
kind, bright and polite. They'd all be lies; but I could say them.

To our roastee:
In my book he's a perfect gentleman, handsome, a scholar, as honest as the day is long...but my book is fiction.

To this occasion:
It's appropriate that we give our friend a dinner—everyone does. She gambles away all her money and hasn't picked up a check in years. Without us, she would starve.

To the big guy:
They wanted to have him roasted by a close friend—but they couldn't find one, so I came instead.

To you, my good friend:
We wanted to give you something you really need, but we couldn't figure out how to wrap an enema.

To our favorite sister:
We thought it would be good to get together and say nice things about her. But then we thought about how much she likes the truth, so we are having this roast.

To the idiot of honor:
A lot of wonderful things have been said about you tonight. Which means the people here are very dumb, very good liars, or you're paying them.

We wanted to give you a piece of the office. We clearly can't give you the elevator, but we can make sure you get the shaft.

Here's to seeing you out in public:
It's so rare. Is your cage being cleaned?

Roast—Returning Fire

To my friends:
I want to come up with a response to your comments that you will understand, that's on your level—about third grade. So, now pay attention. "Stick and stones may break my bones, but names will never hurt me. Nay-nay-a-boo-boo."

To you guys who are trying to roast me:
That makes me a big ham. And it makes you, I guess, flammable gas!

To you guys, for your courage:
You people don't have enough fire power to roast a peanut! The idea of you trying to roast me is like an ant trying to make love to an elephant. If I feel anything at all, I'll be tickled.

To all those who wish to roast me, I have just one piece of advice: Remember that when you point a finger, three fingers are pointing back at you.

Here's to you:
I've taught you well.
You may be smart.
But you still smell.

Here's to my peers: Too bad none of them showed up.

Safe Return Party
See Homecoming (page 82).

Sailing Regatta
Some of my earliest toasting experiences came at a yacht club where the bartender was notorious for his "heavy hand" when pouring drinks. The people dressed for dinner sat in one part of the bar, and the people still crusted with salt from sailing sat in another. In the sailors' section, the tradition of long-form toasting with the lyrics of works such as "Barnacle Bill" and "Keeper of the Light" was occasionally still practiced after a few drinks.

May the ships at sea never be...bottoms up.

Down the hatch!

May your ship never luff.

Bottoms up!

Any port in a storm.

St. Patrick's Day

In addition to the toasts here, you may find some other fitting toasts in the Irish Toasting section of International Toasts (Chapter 9).

For each petal on the shamrock
This brings a wish your way—
Good health, good luck, and happiness
For today and every day.

May your heart be warm and happy
With the lilt of Irish laughter
Every day in every way
And forever and ever after.

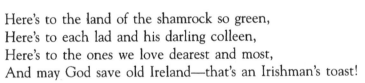

Now sweetly lies old Ireland
Emerald green beyond the foam,
Awakening sweet memories,
Calling the heart back home.

Here's to the land of the shamrock so green,
Here's to each lad and his darling colleen,
Here's to the ones we love dearest and most,
And may God save old Ireland—that's an Irishman's toast!

May your thoughts be as glad as the shamrocks.
May your heart be as light as a song.
May each day bring you bright happy hours,
That stay with you all year long.

May the luck of the Irish
Lead you to new heights
And the roads you travel
Have only green lights!

St. Patrick was a gentleman
Who, through strategy and stealth,
Drove all the snakes from Ireland.
Here's toasting to his health!
But not too many toastings
Lest you lose yourself and then
Forget the good St. Patrick
And see all those snakes again.

May the Irish hills caress you.
May her lakes and rivers bless you.
May the luck of the Irish enfold you.
May the blessings of Saint Patrick behold you.

May the leprechauns be near you,
To spread luck along your way.
And may all the Irish angels,
Smile upon you St. Patrick's Day.

May the luck of the Irish possess you.
May the devil fly off with your worries.
May God bless you forever and ever.

Sales Rally

I love sales people. Despite popular perceptions, they are among the most honest people there are. You know exactly what they want to do: sell you something. More to the point, many salespeople (or sales consultants, if you insist) are champion toasters.

> Business genius Peter Drucker said that "There are no dumb customers." I agree. But there sure are some dumb prospects. Here's to the customers.

> Here's to us! Never sell a salesperson short.

> In the words of Robert Louis Stevenson, "Everyone lives by selling something."So let's keep selling and living. Cheers!

> As P. T. Barnum said, "There's a sucker born every minute."

> Here's to opening accounts and closing deals!

> Here's to the pressure we face:
> For it is, after all, pressure that turns coal into diamonds.

> Here's to making our numbers!

School Function

No matter how much you hated it, the odds are that school did you some good. If you hadn't learned to read, for example, this book would be much less enjoyable. Show your classmates your class by proposing a toast or two.

Let us not forget the words of Oscar Wilde who said, "Education is an admirable thing, but it is well to remember from time to time that nothing worth knowing can be taught."

In the words of Oliver Goldsmith,
"Let schoolmasters puzzle their brains
With grammar and nonsense and learning;
Good liquor I stoutly maintain,
Gives genius a better discerning."

To the grand endeavor of education:
Education pays, they say, but it certainly doesn't pay the educators well!

To education, which Will and Ariel Durant defined as "The transmission of civilization."

Socrates believed that "There is only one good—knowledge; and only one evil—ignorance." Let's toast the fact that this school has made us better.

To my classmates:
As Ralph Waldo Emerson said, "You send your child to the schoolmaster, but 'tis the schoolboys who educate him."

Franklin D. Roosevelt said, "We cannot always build the future for our youth, but we can build our youth for the future." Here's to the future! It's looking very good now, thanks to this school.

George Bernard Shaw said, "What we want is to see the child in pursuit of knowledge, and not knowledge in pursuit of the child." Here's to that great pursuit.

Bernard Berenson said, "Against human nature one cannot legislate. One can only try to educate it." Here's to education.

Benjamin Disraeli said, "A university should be a place of light, of liberty, and of learning." Here's to our alma mater, which meets this definition.

Lyndon B. Johnson said, "The idea of a college education for all young people of capacity, provided at nominal cost by their own states, is very peculiarly American. We in America invented the idea. We in America have developed it with remarkable speed." Here's to education and to America!

Service Awards/Dinner
see Tribute (page 114).

Smokers' Dinner

Smoking and toasting are traditional pastimes; no one would have set a table for some of our grandfathers' without an ashtray or two. Today, fewer people smoke, and there are fewer places where you can smoke. But on those occasions when smokers gather, there are now often women at the table as well as men.

Divine in hookas, glorious in pipe,
When tipped with amber, mellow, rich, and ripe;
Like other charmers, wooing the caress
Most dazzlingly when daring in full dress;
Yet thy true lovers more admire by far
Thy naked beauties—Give me a cigar.
—Lord Byron

Here's to my pipe, a trusty friend indeed,
Filled with that soothing and rest giving weed,
That fills my soul with peace and joy and laughter—
I'd rather smoke here than in the hereafter.

Here's to Kipling who said, "A woman is only a woman, but a good cigar is a smoke."

Sports Awards/Tour/Banquet

You can find a number of useful sports quotes under Athletes and Coaches in Special People (Chapter 4). You may also want to check the quotes in this chapter listed under Victory Celebration and Consolation Party or the toasts listed under Football, Golf, etc.

George Orwell called sports "war minus the shooting." He's right, so let's win. Cheers!

Remember the words of Vince Lombardi, "Winning isn't everything. It's the only thing." Here's to it.

President Warren G. Harding said, "Competition in play teaches the love of the free spirit to excel by its own merit. A nation that has not forgotten how to play, a nation that fosters athletics, is a nation that is always holding up the high ideal of equal opportunity for all. Go back through history and find the nations that did not play and had no outdoor sports, and you will find the nations of oppressed peoples." Here's to American sports.

Here's to the sweet smell of sweaty success.

Store/Office Opening
see Launch (page 85).

Sweet Sixteen

Sweet sixteen parties are one of the sweetest and happiest occasions for some families. They are also a tricky toasting occasion. The young person in question wants it to be clear that they are all grown up, while the older members of the family want it to be clear that this is still their child. It's best to keep the toasts clean and avoid material that might be more appropriate at a bachelor party.

Here's to our baby:
Look how she's grown!
Soon she will be
On her own.

Charles Kingsley said, "Never lose an opportunity of seeing anything beautiful. Beauty is God's handwriting." Here's to our beauty.

Here's to you:
You're so mature,
Soon you'll get a car
You'll have to insure.

Every day you look lovelier and lovelier—and today you look like tomorrow.

To our wonderful sixteen year old:
To us you are more precious than gold.

To quote John Keat's immortal line, "A thing of beauty is a joy forever." Here's to you, beautiful.

You may be sixteen,
But for good or ill,
Remember that
I'm your parent, still.

Team Rally
see also Victory (page 116).

Here's to great ambition,
About which people rant.
It makes you want to do the things
That folks think you can't.

May we always have the class
To rise up off our ass
When there are deeds that must be done
Or novel ways to have fun.

Good, better, best;
Never let it rest,
Till your good is better,
And your better, best.

Here's to doing, not sitting.

To our daring. As they say, "No guts, no glory."

To quote the Nike ad campaign "Just Do It."

"The harder you work, the luckier you get."
—Gary Player

May we be known by our deeds, not by our mortgages.

To action:
As Benjamin Disraeli said, "Action may not always bring happiness, but there is no happiness without action."

Here's to action! In the words of George Bernard Shaw, "You don't learn to hold your own in the world by standing on guard, but by attacking and getting well hammered yourself."

Teetotaler Party

The natural urge to toast is so strong that people will toast with any potable liquid. Those who don't drink alcohol are just as proud of their tastes as those who do, and they announce their preferences with toasts.

May the bloom of the face never extend to the nose.

One swallow doesn't make a summer, but it breaks a New Year's resolution.

To abundance, abstinence, and annihilation:
Abundance to the poor,
Abstinence to the intemperate,
Annihilation to the wicked.

May the beam of the glass never destroy the ray of the mind.

See our glorious banner waving,
Hear the bugle call,
Rally comrades to the standard
Down with alcohol.

Here's to the fall of Bacchus, he's drowned more men than Neptune.

If you drink like a fish,
Drink what a fish drinks.

"We drink to one another's healths and spoil our own."
—Jerome K. Jerome

To moderation in all things—except in love.

May we fly from the temptation we cannot resist.

First the man takes a drink,
Then the drink takes a drink,
Then the drink takes the man.

Here's to wine, wit, and wisdom.
Wine enough to sharpen wit,
Wit enough to give zest to wine,
Wisdom enough to "shut down" at the right time.

To Water:
We never want cash to buy it,
We are never ashamed to ask for it,
And we never blush to drink it."

Here's to a temperance supper
With water in glasses tall,
And coffee and tea to end with
And good health to one and all.

Here's to abstinence:
May it continue to reduce the number of men who think they
can sing.

Our drink shall be water, bright, sparkling with glee,
The gift of our God, and the drink of the free.

Tennis Match

When you are toasting at a tennis club, the best form is still one-handed.

To tennis:
The only excuse that some women get for wearing white.

Here's to tennis:
The sport where love means nothing.

To tennis:
May we all have net gains.

Here's to those who have the guts to be in the tennis racket.

Thanksgiving

Toasts are the perfect format for putting the *thanks* into a Thanksgiving gathering.

Here's to the earth:
Thanks for the harvest.

For what we are about to receive,
may the Lord make us truly thankful.

Here's to the turkey I'm about to eat
and the turkeys I'll eat it with.

Here's to the blessing of the year,
Here's to the friends we hold so dear,
To peace on earth, both far and near.

The American Eagle and the Thanksgiving Turkey,
May one give us peace in all our States,
And the other a piece for all our plates.

Theater/Movie Opening or Wrap

For the record, "break a leg" is a traditional toast to people about to give a performance. It refers to bending one's knee while bowing for applause, and not to fracturing one's tibia.

Break a leg!

To our lines:
May they never be cut.

To the Bard who said, "The play's the thing."

Shakespeare wrote, "All the world's a stage,
And all the men and women merely players:
They have their exits and their entrances;
And one man in his time plays many parts."
May we all play may parts in our time, and get paid for them all!

To the great Tallulah Bankhead who told people, "If you really
want to help the American theater, don't be an actress, dahling.
Be an audience."

To George Burns:
Not only did he stay on stage into his nineties, but he also said,
"Acting is all about honesty. If you can fake that, you've got it
made."

Robert Morley said, "I don't work—I merely inflict myself on the
public." Here's to our being great afflictions.

Tribute

Many toasting occasions are held to honor someone. You may
also find some helpful toasts for a tribute ceremony or celebration in
Special People (Chapter 4).

∞ The "Looking Up" Toast ∞

This toast involves a little acting on your part. It works best at
small gatherings where everyone in the room can see you clearly.
First you ask everyone in the room to stand up. Then you sit
down, or lie on the floor if the room allows and raise your glass
saying, "Here's to everyone I look up to!"

To quote Jonathan Brown, "Whenever the occasion arose, he
rose to the occasion."

Here's to a fellow who smiles
When life runs along like a song.
And here's to the lad who can smile
When everything goes dead wrong.

Here's to you:
Oliver Wendell Holmes said that, "The world's great men have
not commonly been great scholars, nor great scholars great men."
You sure aren't a scholar, so you must be great.

Robert Louis Stevenson said, "that man is a success who has lived
well, laughed often, and loved much; who has gained the respect
of intelligent men and the love of children; who has filled his
niche and accomplished his task; who leaves the world better
than he found it; who never lacked appreciation for the earth's
beauty or failed to express it; who looked for the best in others
and gave the best he had." All this applies to our guest-of-honor.
So here's to him, a true success.

What can we say but, you're our hero!

Lord Barbazon said "Always behave like a duck—keep calm and
unruffled on the surface but paddle like the devil underneath."
Here's to someone who follows that philosophy. He's one duck of
a fellow.

In light of all you've done,
We think you're number one!
Cheers!

Here's to a woman who has so improved her community that she
can say, as the great architect Sir Christopher Wren said, "If you
seek my monument, look around you."

We couldn't like you more,
Here's to more like you.

To someone, who has demonstrated that you can, in fact, teach
an old dog new tricks.

I recognize your remarkable achievements with a line from
Shakespeare's *As You Like It*, "You have deserved high
commendation, true applause, and love."

Your marvels, one by one,
I'd toast without much thinking
But before the tale was well begun
I would be dead from drinking.

To our benefactor:
He came forward when we needed him most, proving the old saying that "when it gets dark enough, you will see the stars."

As Dorothy Parker once said to a friend who had just given birth, "Congratulations: we all knew you had it in you."

Victory Celebration

Victory is something that must be celebrated with a toast or two. Here a few that are sure to be appropriate:

To the profound ignorance, which we brought to this endeavor: Because had we known what was ahead, we never would have started.

Here's to winning! Sure beats losing.

Here's to the sweet smell of success.

Here's to fair play:
Let's try it next time!

Here's to General Douglas MacArthur who said, "There is no substitute for victory."

Here's to what we wanted
When we begun:
The season's over
We're number one.

As Alex Haley said, "History is written by the winners." To victory!

A Toast to the Reader

At every occasion
The person liked most
Is the one who is ready
With a wonderful toast.

Chapter 4

Toasts for Special People

M uch toasting is done to honor special friends. There doesn't
need to be a special occasion, just a special feeling. The
following section may help you find the perfect way to acknowledge
what someone means to you. When in doubt, you can always consider
the toastee a "friend" and use one of the toasts listed under Friends.

Absent Friends

The toast to "Absent Friends" is a tradition among many groups.
In the British Royal Navy, it was a toast traditionally made on Sunday.
"Absent friends" generally refers to people who are still alive, but who
aren't present at the moment.

To our absent friends:
Although they are out of sight, we recognize them with our
glasses.

Here's to our absent friends:
In the hopes that they, wherever they are, are drinking to us.

I was going to make a toast to absent friends...and I suppose I'll
have to include the waiter in that toast.

Here's to absent friends—particularly to prosperity.

Here's to our faraway friends:
May their spirits be with us as soon as these spirits are in us.

Here's to our absent friends:
God bless them.

Here's to absent friends—both the long-lost friends of our youth
and our own long-lost youth.

Here's to the woman I love,
I wish that she were nigh;
If drinking beer would bring her here,
I'd drink the damned place dry.

Here's to the girl I love best,
I picked her out from all the rest;
She's not here to take her part,
So I'll drink to her with all my heart.

Accountants

To my accountant:
May he make many brilliant deductions.

To my accountant:
She brings new meaning to doing it by the numbers.

Let's toast the most calculating person we know!

To our friend the accountant:
May he someday learn what maturity means.

Here's to the accountant:
If we had royalty in America, he'd surely be the Count.

Here's to the accountant—the person who tells you what to do
with your money after you've done something else with it.

To accountants—the people who really know the score in
business.

Advertising Executives

To advertising, which Marshall McLuhan called, "the greatest art form of the twentieth century."

To the modern cowboys—the ones who do all the branding.

May you never forget that 30 seconds may be long on TV, but it's short in the bedroom.

Here's to advertising:
As Stuart Henderson Britt said, "Doing business without advertising is like winking at a girl in the dark. You know what you are doing, but nobody else does."

To big budgets;
In the words of P.T. Barnum, "Advertising is like learning—a little is a dangerous thing."

Here's to H.L. Mencken who said, "No one ever went broke underestimating the taste of the American public."

Here's to the mints—the only places that make money without advertising.

To our sins of commission!

Architects

To the guy who planned the building that holds this bar.

To the architect:
She's lucky we finished the job before the building inspector came around.

To the stud of studs!

Here's to the challenges of being an architect:
To quote Frank Lloyd Wright, "The physician can bury his mistakes, but the architect can only advise his client to plant vines."

To the architect:
In the immortal words of Ambrose Bierce, "one who drafts a plan of your house, and plans a draft of your money."

May you get elevations whenever you want them!

As we architects love to say, "Back to the drawing board."

Here's to the ivy which eventually covers our mistakes.

Artists

To the return of the tradition of patrons.

To the artist, to quote John O'Hara, "An artist is his own fault."

To Michaelangelo, Leonardo, and our friend here.

Let's lift our glasses to the artist, who has just completed a lovely painting—and missed none of the numbers!

May you be hung!

May your work be mounted rightside-up.

Here's to the artist, or in the words of Robert W. Corrigan, "The artist is the seismograph of his age."

Let us all agree that while we might
not know much about art,
we know what we like: the artist.

To your work:
May it speak for itself. Loudly.

To the artists:
Havelock Ellis said it best when he said, "Every artist writes his own autobiography."

May the critics be kind.

Athletes

To those whose bodies are temples:
May you never build an unwanted addition.

To those who think that sweat is sweet.

May you enjoy the three skills of the hare: sharp turning, high jumping, and strong running against the hill.

May you score whenever you want.

To our favorite swinger:
May he always play the field and never be caught off base.

Here's to those who know their goals.

Here's to all those true competitors, or in the immortal words of Vince Lombardi, "Winning isn't everything. It's the only thing."

To a real nice guy and the ultimate athlete:
He's the only one I know who disproves Leo Durocher's famous quote, "Nice guys finish last."

May we build muscles everywhere but in our heads.

Here's hoping that you always play fair. And if you don't, may the officials be looking the other way.

Aunts

When Mom was gone
I barely missed her
Because I had
My Mother's [Father's] sister!

Call her ant
Or call her awnt
She says that you can
When you think you can't.

She shared with me
Family history;
A parent's sister,
But like a sister to me.

Bankers

Here's to the banks:
To quote Mark Twain, "Banks will lend you money if you can
prove you don't need it."

To our banker:
We know our money's safe, because he's forgotten the
combination.

To the banker:
A person who lends you an umbrella on a fair day only to take it
away when it rains.

Here's to the banker:
The man behind most self-made men.

Here's to you. I can truly say, we all owe a debt to you.

To our misguided friend the banker who thought he was going
into a simple, stable profession.

You've given us many statements, now it's time to give one to
you: you're great.

To our friend the banker:
May he never lose interest.

Here's to you, and you alone.
A compliment in a different tone.
We will not beg, we will not moan.
Right now, we're not asking you for a loan!

Benefactors

To a person so generous that it makes me want to say, "Yes, my friends, there is a Santa Claus."

To our benefactor, whose presents make our hearts grow fonder.

Here's a toast to you,
You great big honey!
We can't get enough of you
Or of your money.

No one was funnier
Than Ogden Nash
But you're more memorable
'Cause you give cash!
Here's to you.

To our good friend and benefactor, whose charity never failed us.

Here's to our benefactor, who God must love, for the Bible says, "God loveth a cheerful giver."

I propose that we honor our guest with a toast, for our guest has been truly generous, and, as Calvin Coolidge said "No person was ever honored for what he received. Honor has been the reward for what he gave."

"I've traveled many a highway
I've walked for many a mile
Here's to the people who made my day
To the people who waved and smiled."
—Tom T. Hall

To our benefactor, whose recent generosity has confirmed what we have long suspected—that he is a remarkable person.

Lift 'em high and drain 'em dry
To the guy who says, "My turn to buy!"

"Drink down all unkindness."
—Shakespeare, *The Merry Wives of Windsor*

Here's to riches to the generous and power to the merciful.

May we strengthen the weak, give light to the blind, clothe the naked, and be friends to mankind.

'Tis easy to say "Fill 'em"
When your account's not overdrawn
But the man worthwhile,
Is the man who can smile,
When every damned cent is gone.

Bosses

To our boss:
The star to which we have all hitched our wagon.

Here's to the master of mushroom management:
You keep us in the dark and you feed us manure, but we love you anyway.

Here's to you,
For all you've done;
When it comes to bosses,
You're second to none.

Here's to the guy who had the vision
To start this place despite derision
You built the company up in stages
And never forgot to pay our wages.

Here's to the man who signs our pay checks:
May he never hear what we say about him.

To the boss:
The person who's early when you're late, and late when you're early.

Here's to the woman who makes the rules,
And treats us like we aren't all fools.
I may not like all you do
But there's no one else I'd report to.

May we never flatter our superiors or insult our inferiors.

Here's to bosses and diapers:
Both are always on your butt and usually full of crap.

Here's to our boss:
When he tells you not to worry—start worrying.

Brothers

Here's to cheating, stealing, fighting, and drinking:
If you cheat, may you cheat death.
If you steal, may you steal a woman's heart.
If you fight, may you fight for a brother.
And if you drink, may you drink with me.

To the man who's really happy he has an older brother: Can you imagine how he'd look in his sister's hand-me-downs?

To the 'r' in the word brother:
Without it, you'd just be a bother.

Here's to the bond that comes with having the same parents.

To my brother;
As John Ray said, "Blood is thicker than water."

Builders

Here's to the foundations of our community, and the guys that pour them.

Here's to the man who comes home every day and says his work was riveting.

To building:
The profession where you always start in the hole.

Here's to the heroes who make our homes.

To the brotherhood of hammer and saw.

Children

To the new parents:
They are about to enter a "changing" world!

A generation of children on the children of your children.

To our children, and let us not forget as Joseph Joubert said, they "have more need of models than of critics."

To children—the future of the world.

Here's to children—the truest legacy we leave to the world.

To the children of the world:
May they never go hungry.

To children:
May we be patient with their questions.

To the innocence of children and the inner sense of adults.

Here's to my child:
Someone I've known for his whole life, who, nonetheless, continues to surprise and impress me.

Coaches

Here's to the man who made us winners.

Here's to a prince,
Above all chaps
The guy who makes us
Run all those laps.

Here's to our coach:
A man who's willing to lay down our lives for his school.

Let me make a little pitch
About our favorite son of a bitch
I'll make it short, not go on for hours
If I did, he'd send me to the showers.
Here's to you, coach.

To the man for whom our sweat is sweet.

Let's drink to the coach and hope he doesn't catch us!

Let's wet our whistles in honor of the gal who's blown her whistle at us so often.

May this be just the first of many toasts to the coach. After all, as he says, practice, practice, practice.

Clergy

To our minister:
Who would rather preach than practice.

Here's to a father
Who's never a bother.

Here's to the messenger of peace!

When you get home tonight
Say you were with the rabbi,
He's the man of the hour
And a great alibi!

To our pastor and his divine influence:
As Minister Harry Emerson Fosdick once said, "Preaching is personal counseling on a group basis."

Here's to the guy who wears the collar,
Who shouts in a whisper, instead of a holler,
Who leads so we can foller,
And always asks for that extra dollar!

To the Padre, who, by not drinking, leaves more for us.

Here's to our priest:
In the words of Robert Runcie, Archbishop of Canterbury, "The priest is concerned with other people for the sake of God and with God for the sake of other people."

To the guy who, literally, gets us reading from the same prayer book.

Cousins

To my cousins:
Because of you, I never felt like an only child.

Here's to cousins:
Kissing and otherwise.

To our clan
The best there are
Every woman
Every man.

To my many cousins who always made it seem that everything is relative.

To my overseas cousins:
As John Ray said, "Blood is thicker than water."

Critics

To the brave critic:
Here's a soul who knows his taste,
Who with clear opinion is graced.
It's not that he reviews in haste,
He has no time or words to waste.

To the critic:
Someone who likes to write about things he doesn't like.

To our critics:
I offer the wise words of Benjamin Disraeli who said, "It is much easier to be critical than to be correct."

To our critics I give the words of Rudolf Bing who said, "I am perfectly happy to believe that nobody likes us but the public."

To the critic's patron saint, Harry S. Truman, to whom these immortal words are attributed: "If you can't stand the heat, you'd better get out of the kitchen."

To she who needs neither meat nor heat to create a stew. Just a few choice lines in a review.

Dentists

To the man who deals with the tooth, the whole tooth and nothing but the tooth!

To the man we call Novocaine, because he's so painless.

Let us give our friend a hearty toast:
We'd give him a plaque, but he'd just scrape it away.

To the dentist:
The person who runs a filling station and is a collector of old magazines.

Here's to the dentist who got most of his training in the military—as a drill sergeant.

To the dentist:
He makes his living hand to mouth.

To the professional who knows
the gravity of every cavity,
and the truth of every tooth.

To a guy who really gets to the root of things!

Doctors

When in doubt, refer to a medical doctor as a "physician" in your toast. They seem to prefer this term, perhaps because it distinguishes them from "academic" doctors. However, if you know the person well, feel free to call him or her "Doctor."

Physician's Toast:
To mankind we drink: 'Tis a pleasant task.
Heaven bless it and multiply its wealth;
But it is a little too much to ask
That we should drink to its health.

To our friend who manages to care despite managed care.

You give us shots
When we have spots.
And prescribe pills
When we have chills.
You poke and prod
Each and every bod
So here's something new
We're giving health to you!

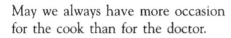

May we always have more occasion
for the cook than for the doctor.

In the words of Philip McAllister,
"Unto our doctors let us drink,
Who cure our chills and ills,
No matter what we really think
About their pills and bills."

Let's lift our glasses to the doctor:
A person to whom we trust our lives and our fortunes.

Here's to those who heal!

Here's to a great physician:
The only one I know who thinks a dressing is something you put
on a salad.

Ah, drugs! To quote William Osler, "The desire to take medicine
is perhaps the greatest feature which distinguishes man from
animals."

Here's to precision, decision, and incision!

Farmers

Here's to a man who rarely rests
Because he's dealing with the pests.

Here's to farmers:
People who are always out standing in their fields.

To a man who loves to toil
And bring food from our soil:
Please never stop,
We eat that crop!

To our fields:
May they go to seed.

To America's farms:
They feed the world.

In the words of E. B. White, "A good farmer is nothing more nor less than a handy man with a sense of humus."

Fathers

To the new father:
Good luck as you enter a "changing" world.

To dad:
May the love and respect we express toward him make up for the worry and care we have visited upon him.

To my father:
If I can become half the man he is, I'll have achieved greatness.

Fathers hold their children's hands for just a little while, and their hearts forever.

Friends

Many toasts are given to friends and almost anyone you propose a toast to becomes, to one degree or another, a friend. You can also find more toasts for friends in Best Wishes Toasts (Chapter 5).

Here is a note we received from our friend Lori in Florida. It shows how important toasting friends can be, especially at holiday time.

"I remember reading an article many years ago entitled, "Friends Are the New Family." Never having married nor had children, and always living on the other side of the country (and sometimes the other side of the world) from what little family I have left, I have come to understand the meaning of that phrase in a very personal way. My holidays, since 1963, have been spent primarily with friends. Some have been there for only a few celebrations. Many have been present for almost all of them. We have shared crises and triumphs and furnished each other much love and support over the years. We have created holiday customs and traditions that are now long-standing. We have a list of standard calls we make to those who are missing. One tradition, our Christmas dinner toast, recognizes the importance of these friendships. We toast "To Friends, Present and Absent, and to our *Hoops of Steel.*" The toast is derived from a portion of Polonius' Advice to his Son in Shakespeare's *Hamlet.* Many remember the end of the speech which begins, "This above all, to thine own self be true...." Our toast comes from one of the previous sections which says: "Those friends thou hast and their adoption tried, grapple them to thy soul with hoops of steel..." We toast the 'hoops of steel,' tempered over the years, that have brought us so much joy and comfort."

To my friends:
Friends we are today,
And friends we'll always be—
For I am wise to you,
And you can see through me.

The test of Gold is Fire.
The test of Truth is Time.
The test of God's love are the heavens above
and everything sublime.
Treasures in life are many, dreams realized but few.
But I know the proof of God's goodness
is when he gave me a friend like you.

To friends: As long as we are able
To lift our glasses from the table.

God gives us our relatives:
Thank God, we can choose our friends.

May we never want a friend to cheer us, or a bottle to cheer him.

When friends with other friends contrive
To make their glasses clink,
Then not one sense of all the five
Is absent from the drink.

For touch and taste and smell and sight
Evolve in pleasant round,
And when the flowing cups unite
We thrill to sense of sound.
Folly to look on wine? Oh fie
On what the teetotalers think...
There's five good reasons why
Good fellows like to drink.

Here's to the best key for unlocking friendship—whiskey.

To quote George Sterling,
"He who clinks his cup with mine
Adds a glory to the wine."

Good-bye, dear ones, and if you need a friend,
How happy I will be,
Should you get tired of life's rough way
Just come and lean on me.

I'll take you on the smoothest road that God to man e'er gave;
And will go by the longest way that takes us to the grave.

Here's to the man who is wisest and best.
Here's to the man who with judgment is blest.
Here's to the man who's as smart as can be—
I drink to the man who agrees with me!

Here's to one sweetheart, one bottle, and one friend:
The first beautiful, the second full, and the last ever faithful.

Here's to cold nights, warm friends, and a good drink to give
them.

I'd rather have dinner when I'm living than a monument when I'm dead, for the dinner will be on my friends, while the monument would be on me.

A glass is good, and a lass is good,
And a warm hearth in cold weather,
The world is good and people are good,
And we're all good people together.

Nothing but the best for you. That's why you have us as friends.

A health to you,
A wealth to you,
And the best that life can give to you.
May fortune still be kind to you,
And happiness be true to you,
And life be long and good to you,
Is the toast of all your friends to you.

Don't walk in front of me,
I may not follow.
Don't walk behind me,
I may not lead.
Walk beside me,
And just be my friend.

Friendship's the wine of life.
Let's drink of it and to it.

May the friends of our youth be the companions of our old age.

In the words of Tom Moore, "Pour deep the rosy wine and drink a toast with me: Here's to the three: Thee, Wine, and Camaraderie."

The world is happy and colorful,
And life itself is new.
And I am very grateful for
The friend I found in you.

To our best friends, who hear the worst about us but refuse to believe it.

Forsake not an old friend, for the new is not comparable to him. A new friend is as new wine: When it is old, thou shalt drink it with pleasure. *Ecclesiastes* 9:10

To good byes: that they never be spoken.
To friendships: may they never be broken.

Love to one, friendship to a few, and goodwill to all.

When climbing the hill of prosperity, may we never meet a friend coming down.

May we have a few real friends rather than a thousand acquaintances.

May we never have friends who, like shadows, keep close to us in the sunshine, only to desert us on a cloudy day.

May friendship, like wine, improve as time advances, and may we always have old wine, old friends, and young cares.

Here's to the friends of tomorrow.

"May the hinges of friendship never rust, nor the wings of love lose a feather."
—Dean Ramsay

Here's to friendship:
One soul in two bodies.

Here's to the tears of friendship:
May they crystallize as they fall and be worn as jewels by those we love.

May we treat our friends with kindness and our enemies with generosity.

To a true friend:
One before whom I can think aloud.

To a true friend:
She knows all about me and loves me just the same.

A health to our sweethearts, our friends, and our wives,
And may fortune smile on them the rest of their lives.

To a friend who remembers all the details of our childhood, and has the discretion not to mention them.

To you, the second most supportive element in my life. I wish I could say you were the most supportive, but at my age, I'm not about to go braless.

To my friends, who have proved to me the meaning of Cicero's observation that "In friendship we find nothing false or insincere; everything is straightforward and springs from the heart."

To our misspent youth:
May our children never be half as rowdy.

To our friends who keep city life from being what Henry David Thoreau called it: "Millions of people being lonesome together."

To perfect friends who were once perfect strangers.

May you have more and more friends, and need them less and less.

Here's to us:
As Shakespeare said, "Good company, good wine, good welcome, make good people."

In all this world, why I do think
There are four reasons why we drink?
Good friends,
Good wine,
Lest we be dry
and any other reason why!

May you never lie, steal, cheat, or drink.
But if you must lie, lie in each other's arms.
If you must steal, steal kisses.
If you must cheat, cheat death.
And if you must drink, drink with us, your friends.

One bottle for four of us—thank God there's no more of us!

Here's to the true hinges of Friendship—
Swearing, Lying, Stealing, and Drinking.
When you swear, swear by your country;
When you lie, lie for a pretty woman;
When you steal, steal away from bad company;
And when you drink, drink with me.

Here's to Eternity: May we spend it in as good company as this night finds us.

To our friendship, which, like the wine in this glass, has mellowed and gotten better and better over time.

To our humorous friend: May you always be healthy, wealthy, and wisecracking.

Here's to you: You may not be as wise as an owl, but you're always a hoot.

To all those who tolerated us as we grew up, and all those who tolerate us now.

"Old wood to burn, old wine to drink,
old friends to trust, and old authors to read."
—Francis Bacon

Happy are we met, happy have we been,
Happy may we part, and happy meet again.

May we ever be able to serve a friend and noble enough to conceal it.

"Oh! Be thou blest with that heaven can send,
Long health, long youth, long pleasure—and a friend."
—Alexander Pope

"If I do vow a friendship, I'll perform it to the last article."
—William Shakespeare, *Othello*

Here's to those who love us well,
Those who don't can go to Hell.

Here's to our absent friends; although out of sight, we recognize them with our glasses.

To our friends:
May their joy be as deep as the ocean, their troubles as light as its foam.

May thy life be long and happy,
Thy cares and sorrows few;
And the many friends around thee
Prove faithful, fond, and true.

May our injuries be written in sand and our friendships in marble.

To my friend, for proving that Ibsen was wrong when he said, "A friend married is a friend lost."

I salute my long-time friend in the words of La Fontaine who said, "Friendship is the shadow of the evening which strengthens with the setting sun of life."

Here's to the friend
Who listens to my advice,
Who rejoices in my success,
Who scorns my enemies,
Who laughs at my jokes,
Who ignores my ignorance.

Wine, to strengthen friendship and light the flame of love.

"Here's to the fellow who smiles,
While life rolls on like a song,
And here's to a chap who can smile,
When everything goes dead wrong."

Grandchildren

To our grandchildren: Our revenge on our children!

Here's to our grandchildren. May they always carry our name proudly.

Here's to Grandchildren: God's way of compensating us for growing old.

To our grandchildren: May we not spoil them *too* much.

Here's to grandchildren—and the joy of seeing our family enter another generation.

Grandparents

Here's to grandparents:
The cheapest (and best) babysitters on earth.

To the greatest grandparents:
May they live to be great-grandparents.

Let us raise our glasses
And then imbibe
To the splendid couple
Who founded this tribe.

To my children's grandparents:
The people behind the new G.I. plan—Generous In-laws!

Guests

A guest is a special kind of friend, so if you don't find a toast you like here, look under Friends (page 132). You can also look in Best Wishes (Chapter 5).

In the truly immortal words of Bram Stoker's Count Dracula, "Welcome to my house. Come freely. Go safely. And leave something of the happiness you bring!"

Here's a toast to all who are here,
No matter where you're from;
May the best day you have seen
Be worse than your worst to come.

Here's to our guest—don't let him rest.
But keep his elbow bending.
'Tis time to drink—full time to think
Tomorrow, when you're mending.

To our guests:
Our house is ever at your service.

In the words of Myrtle Reed, "May our house always be too small to hold all our friends."

"The ornament of a house is the guests who frequent it."
—Ralph Waldo Emerson

By the bread and salt, by the water and wine,
You are welcome, friends, at this table of mine.

"Come in the evening, or come in the morning—
Come when you're looked for, or come without warning;
A thousand welcomes you'll find here before you,
The oftener you come here the more I'll adore you."
—Thomas O. Davis

"Good company, good wine, good welcome, make good people."
—Shakespeare

As Thomas Lipton once said, "Here's to all of us."

You are welcome here
For a short, pleasant stay.
But guests, like fish,
Are not good the third day!

Here's a health to thee and thine
From the hearts of me and mine;
And when thee and thine
Come to see me and mine,
May me and mine make thee and thine
As welcome as thee and thine
Have ever made me and mine.

Hosts

We know we'll have fun,
And no reason to grouse,

Whenever we visit,
The folks in this house.

To our host, a most excellent man:
For is not a man fairly judged by the company he keeps?

Here's to your welcome which was cordial, and your cordial
which is welcome.

There are few folks
Who would ever be able
To put out the spread
We see on this table.

Here's to the hostess and host,
Jolly good health in this toast.
May your journey be good
On the road that you choose
Though it be fast or slow
And joy attend you all the way
Whichever road you go.

To our hostess:
She's a gem. We love her. God bless her.
And the devil take her husband.

To our host who gives us what Henry Sambrooke Leigh described
as, "The rapturous, wild, and ineffable pleasure of drinking at
somebody else's expense."

What's a table richly spread
Without this woman at its head?

Here's a toast to our host from all of us;
May he soon be the guest of each of us.

Here's to our hostess, considerate and sweet;
Her wit is endless, but when do we eat?

To the sun that warmed the vineyard,
To the juice that turned to wine,
To the host that cracked the bottle,
And made it yours and mine.

To our friend, who is neither an optimist who sees a glass as half full, nor a pessimist who sees a glass as half empty; but a host, who sees it as a glass that needs topping off.

Let us raise our glasses high and thank our host for the pleasure of being his company.

To our host, who has the ability to make us all feel at home, even though that's where he wishes we were.

To our hostess with the most-ess.

Here's a toast to the host who carved the roast;
And a toast to the hostess: May she never roast us.

Here's to the hostess and here's to the host,
As we raise up our glasses and offer this toast;
Thank you for this lovely meal,
Thank you for these friends so real,
Thank you for the way we feel.
We think you're just the most.

To our host:
Happiness, health, and prosperity.

Here's to the bride
And here's to the groom
And to the bride's father
Who'll pay for this room.

Husbands

To the first man who could win both my heart and my mother's approval.

Here's to a man who loves his wife, and loves his wife alone.
For many a man loves another man's wife, when he ought to be loving his own.

To the model husband—any other woman's!

Here's to the man who is wisest and best,
Here's to the man whose judgment is blest.
Here's to the man who's as smart as can be—
I mean the man who agrees with me.

To my husband, a man of few words.

To our sweethearts and husbands:
May they never meet!

Here's to the husband who can bravely say,
"I have loved her, all my life—
Since I took her hand on the wedding day
I have only loved my wife."

A good husband and health
Are a woman's best wealth.

Lawyers

Note that some lawyers enjoy being referred to as a friend as much as they like to be recognized as a lawyer. Evidently, it can be a rare experience for some of them.

Here's to the law:
A bad compromise beats a good lawsuit.

To the man who is always right for the case!

"And do as adversaries in law—
Strive mightily, but eat and drink as friends."
—Shakespeare, *The Taming of the Shrew*

To our lawyer:
No matter his age, he's always courting!

"A bumper of good liquor
Will end a contest quicker
Than justice, judge, or vicar;
So fill a cheerful glass,
and let good humor pass."
—Richard B. Sheridan

To our friend who's proud of his briefs.

In the words of Charles Macklin, to "The glorious uncertainty of the law."

In Shakespeare's immortal words from *Henry VI*, "Kill all lawyers."

To the lawyer who knows it's often better to know the judge than it is to know the law.

Here's to the vanguards of the medical and legal professions, as they say,
Fond of doctors, little health;
Fond of lawyers, little wealth.

Here's a toast to a man of great trials and many convictions.

Here's to the lawyer:
A bright gentleman, who rescues your estate from your enemies, and keeps it for himself.

To lawyers:
In the words of Joseph H. Choate, "You cannot live without the lawyers, and certainly you cannot die without them."

Here's to the advice my lawyer gave me:
Say it with flowers,
Say it with eats,
Say it with kisses,
Say it with sweets,
Say it with jewelry,
Say it with drink,
But always be careful
Not to say it with ink.

Mothers

To the mother who bore me,
There's no one more bold,
She's dearer by far
Than all of earth's gold.

Mothers hold their children's hands for just a little while...and their hearts forever.

To our mothers—God bless them every one
May the eyes of the Fathers and the love of the Sons
Watch over and protect them, keep them holy and pure,
With life to sustain and health to endure.

We have toasted our sweethearts,
Our friends and our wives,
We have toasted each other
Wishing all merry lives;
Don't frown when I tell you
This toast beats all others
But drink one more toast, boys—
A toast to our mothers.

Here's to the happiest hours of my life
Spent in the arms of another man's wife—
My mother!

It's not the woman with ebon locks,
Nor the one with head of brown,
Or the lady fair with the golden hair,
Or the one with the copper crown.
But the woman I love the best of all,
And the one I toast tonight,
With her smiling face and easy grace,
Wears a mane of shimmering white:
My mother.

To our father's sweethearts: our mothers.

To our mothers and all that they have meant to us. They are the proof of the Jewish proverb that "God could not be everywhere, so he made mothers."

Mothers-in-Law

Here's to my mother-in-law who let me take her baby from her...without too much of a fight.

To my mother-in-law who has finally stopped regarding me as the outlaw.

Here's to the mother-in-law, because as Brooks Hays once said, "Behind every successful man stands a proud wife and a surprised mother-in-law."

Parents

To my parents who have spoiled me my whole life long: Don't stop!

To our children:
Let us not forget what Joseph Joubert said, they "have more need of models than of critics."

To the new parents:
They will learn, as I did, about babies, that you've got to love them. Unfortunately, you also have to feed them and change them, too. Good luck.

Here's to my parents:
Two people who spent half their time wondering how I'd turn out, and the rest of the time when I'd turn in.

Raise a glass to those who raised us.

It is written that when children find true love, parents find true joy. Here's to your joy and ours, from this day forward.

Politicians

Here's to politicians:
The distiller's true friend.
For wherever you find four politicians together
You're sure to find a fifth.

Here's to the honest politician who, as defined by Simon Cameron, "when he is bought, will stay bought."

To the politician:
A person who divides his time between running for office and running for cover.

Here's to our politician:
A man who stands for what he thinks others will fall for.

To our newly elected officials:
May they do only a minimal amount of damage this session.

To our flag, long may it wave.
And to our politicians, long may they rave!

Give us pure candidates and a pure ballot box,
And our freedom shall stand as firm as the rocks.

Professors

To the woman who is driving the academic epidemic!

To the professor:
A man who talks in his students' sleep.

To the Dean:
Who does well despite his faculties.

His lectures are so perfect,
There's rarely a cough
And exams are open-book
That's why we like our Prof.

H. L. Mencken said that "A professor must have a theory as a dog must have fleas." And he had never even met our prof!

To my professor: a textbook wired for sound.

The world's full of adversity
And hatred and perversity
And that's just what we've found
While at the University!
To our professor...

To our professor:
A person whose job it was to tell us how to solve the problems of life which he himself had avoided by becoming a professor.

To our professor:
Addition to your friends,
Subtraction from wants,
Multiplication of your blessings,
Division among your foes.

"Let schoolmasters puzzle their brain
With grammar and nonsense and learning;
Good liquor, I stoutly maintain,
Gives genius a better discerning."
—Oliver Goldsmith

Psychiatrists & Psychologists

First, you should ask yourself why you want to toast this person. What feelings does he or she bring up in you? Why are you so concerned with how they feel about you? Hmm. What do you think? That will be $60.

Some call them "Shrinks," but I prefer Gene Moore's term of "Stretches." Here's to the guy who expands our horizons.

To the psychiatrist who Mervyn Stockwood defines as, "a man who goes to the Follies-Bergere and looks at the audience."

To the psychiatrist:
He may not solve your problems, but he'll tell you how to couch them.

To the psychologist:
He finds you cracked and leaves you broke.

Here's to our psychologist:
We're so glad your first career didn't work out.

Let's drink to the psychiatrist:
Someone whose patients take their medicine lying down.

Prozac, Zoloft, Elavil,
We've got the pills.
But we need you still!

Here's to my shrink, who doesn't understand me.

To the psychologist:
He's even managed to convince himself that he knows what he's talking about.

To the shrink:
The shoemaker's kids go shoeless.
And *your* kids . . .
Well, here's to you.

Here's to the psychiatrist:
A person who doesn't have to worry as long as other people do.

Salespeople

You never rest,
You never slumber,
Up until
You've made your number.
Here's to you!

To a great salesperson:
Some make trouble,
Others make excuses and you make good.

In the words of Kermit the Frog, "Sell, Sell, Sell."

Here's to P.T. Barnum who said, "There's a sucker born every moment."

Everyone is selling something. Here's to someone who is open about it.

Here's to us:
Never sell a salesperson short.

Here's to a lady who's covered in glory,
Every inch of her territory.

Sisters

To my sister, whom I forgive:
Some part of every family tree has to be out on a limb.

To my sisters and the secrets we share!

To my sister:
We share parents—but not much else.

We've toasted the mother and the daughter;
We've toasted the sweetheart and wife;
But somehow we missed her,
Our dear little sister—
The joy of another man's life.

Speakers

We'll bless our toastmaster,
Wherever he may roam,
If he'll only cut the speeches short
And let us all go home.

Some will scream and some will squawk
Here's to the man with the nerve to talk.

To our speaker:
May he rise to the occasion, and sit down soon thereafter.

Most people would rather wrestle a bear than speak to a group.
Here's to a woman of real courage, our speaker.

To our speaker, I give the wisdom of Horace who said,
"Whatever advice you give, be brief."

Here's to our speaker:
May his speech be like a pencil and have a point.

Stockbrokers

Here's to the lady who does our shares!

Here's to the stockbroker:
May your life be full of bulls!

To the bonds between us, and the stocks, too.

To my broker:
My feelings for you, like the investments you put me in, are
mostly mutual.

To the stockbroker:
A capitalist who invests himself with other people's money.

May you never forget that bulls and bears can win,
but pigs and sheep get slaughtered.

Teachers

To our teacher:
A person whose job it was to tell us how to solve the problems of
life which he himself had avoided by becoming a teacher.

Jacques Barzun said "Teaching is not a lost art, but regard for it is
a lost tradition." We have before us a great practitioner of the art
of teaching, so let's revive the tradition of respect with a toast.
On your feet and glasses up!

In ancient times, Cicero asked, "What nobler employment, or
more valuable to the state, than that of the man who instructs
the rising generation?" Here's to our teacher.

Oprah Winfrey said, "For every one of us that succeeds, it's
because there's somebody there to show you the way out. The
light doesn't necessarily have to be in your family; for me it was
teachers and school." Let's all thank our teachers with a toast.

Joseph Addison said, "I consider a human soul without education
like marble in a quarry, which shows none of its inherent beauties
until the skill of the polisher sketches out the colors, makes the

surface shine, and discovers every ornamental cloud, spot, and vein that runs through it." Here's to the teachers who sculpted us. They made us beautiful marble, without losing their marbles.

John Locke pointed out that "It is one thing to show a man that he is in error, and another to put him in possession of truth." We salute you for being so gentle with our errors and so focused on our discovery.

Erich Fromm said, "Education is helping the child realize his potentialities." Here's to those who have helped me become what I am today.

John Sculley noted that, "We expect teachers to handle teenage pregnancy, substance abuse, and the failings of the family. Then we expect them to educate our children." It's an impossible task. Thanks for doing it.

Uncles

Four blessings upon you...
Older whiskey,
Younger women,
Faster horses,
More money.

Thanks for the booze you let me sample—
You are my favorite bad example.

From going fishing
To playing "kick the can"
You taught me what I know about being a man.
Here's to you!

Most people think that when they "cry uncle" they are giving in. But thanks to you, whenever I "cried uncle" I have gotten the help I needed to win. Here's to you.

Wives

To my wife: my bride and joy.

To my wife and our anniversary, which I forgot once, but will never forget again.

Here's to our wives:
May they be as blissfully trustful as we are trustfully blissful.

Here's to our wives!
They keep our hives
In little bees and honey;
They darn our socks,
They soothe life's shocks,
And don't they spend the money!

A health to our widows. If they ever marry again, may they do as well!

I know the thing that's most uncommon;
(Envy be silent and attend)
I know a reasonable woman,
Handsome, and witty, yet a friend.
—Alexander Pope

A good wife and health
Are a man's best wealth.

Here's to the wife I love,
And here's to the wife who loves me,
And here's to all those who love her whom I love
And all those who love her who love me.

A health to our sweethearts, our friends and our wives,
And may fortune smile on them the rest of their lives.

Here's to our sweethearts and our wives;
May our sweethearts soon become our wives,
And our wives ever remain our sweethearts.

Here's to the pretty woman,
I fought to marry at all cost.
The struggle was well worth it,
Cause without her I'd be lost.

To my wife:
Here's to the prettiest, here's to the wittiest,
Here's to the truest of all who are true,
Here's to the nearest one, here's to the sweetest one,
Here's to them, all in one—here's to you.

A Toast to the Reader

Here's to you
Not for how you look
But because you
have my book.

Chapter 5

Best Wishes Toasts

There's no reason to save the wonderful custom of toasting for special occasions. Much of the time, you'll want to propose a toast just to show how happy you are at the moment, and use your toast to make the occasion special. It's been said that the best toasts are dedicated to a person or group or cause and that they include a heartfelt wish. You can make almost any of the toasts below sound even more heartfelt by adding the words "because we love you" at the end.

Here are a number of toasts you can make to people or groups that contain wonderful wishes. Don't be shy about including yourself in the group. Part of the magic of toasting is the way it can bring people together. Toasts for best wishes often contain friendly advice, but rarely criticism.

May your troubles be less
And your blessings be more.
And nothing but happiness
Come through your door.

Bless you and yours
As well as the cottage you live in.
May the roof overhead be well thatched
And those inside be well matched.

To the good old days, which we are having right now.

When this life is over, may all of us find peace.

May the Lord love us but not call us too soon.

May you enter heaven late.

Long life to you and may you die in your bed.

May you live to be a hundred and decide the rest for yourself.

May you die in bed at age ninety-five shot by the jealous husband of a teenage wife.

Blessings on your posterity.

May we never be influenced by jealousy nor governed by interest.

Here's to love, life, and liberty:
Love pure,
Life long,
Liberty boundless.

"Laugh and be merry together, like brothers akin,
Guesting awhile in the room of a beautiful inn.
Glad till the dancing stops, and the lilt of the music ends.
Laugh till the game is played; and be you merry my friends."
—John Masefield, from Laugh and Be Merry

To the ladies: God bless them,
May nothing distress them.

Success to the lover,
Honor to the brave,
Health to the sick,
Freedom to the slave.

Here's to health and prosperity,
To you and all your posterity.
And them that doesn't drink with sincerity,
That they may be damned for all eternity!

May your right hand always
Be stretched out in friendship
And never in want.

May the roof above us never fall in.
And may the friends gathered below it never fall out.

May the grass grow long on the road to hell for want of use.

May your bank account always be bigger than your troubles.

May you get all your wishes but one,
so you always have something to strive for!

Moderation is a fatal thing:
Nothing succeeds like excess.
—Oscar Wilde

છ

There are only two things to worry about:
Either you are well or you are sick.
If you are well, then there is nothing to worry about.

But if you are sick, there are two things to worry about:
Either you will get well or you will die.
If you get well, then there is nothing to worry about.

But if you die, there are two things to worry about:
Either you will go to heaven or you will go to hell.
If you go to heaven, then you have nothing to worry about.

But if you go to hell, you'll be so damn busy shaking hands
with all your friends, then you won't have time to worry!

છ

As you ramble through life, whatever be your goal;
Keep your eye upon the doughnut, and not upon the hole.

May you taste the sweetest pleasures that fortune ere bestowed,
and may all your friends remember all the favors you are owed.

May misfortune follow you the rest of your life, but never catch
up.

May the winds of fortune sail you,
May you sail a gentle sea,
May it always be the other guy
who says, "this drink's on me."

May the hinges of our friendship never grow rusty.

May you never dance in a small boat.

"Here's to those who wish us well,
As for the rest, they can go to Hell!"

May your boats never be bottoms up.

Here's health to those I love, and wealth to those who love me.

Health to our sweethearts, our friends, and our wives;
And may fortune smile on them the rest of their lives.

Here's to your health, and your family's good health, and may you
live long and prosper.

To the three H's: Health, Honor, and Happiness.
Health to the world,
Honor to those who seek for it,
Happiness in our homes.

Here's to your health:
A long life and an easy death to you.

Here's to your health!
You make age curious, time furious, and all of us envious.

Here's to health, peace, and prosperity;
May the flower of love never be nipped by the frost of
disappointment, nor the shadow of grief fall among a member of
this circle.

Here's to your health:
May God bring you luck
And may your journey be smooth and happy.

To your health:
May we drink one together in ten years time and a few in
between.

Here's to health to your soul and health to your heart;
Where this is going, there's gone many a quart.
Through my teeth and round my gums;
Look out, belly, here it comes.

To you, and yours, and theirs, and mine:
I pledge with you, their health in wine.

Here's health to all who need it.

I drink to your health when I'm with you,
I drink to your health when I'm alone,
I drink to your health so often
I'm beginning to worry about my own.

To your very good health. May you live to be as old as your jokes.

"I drink to the general joy of the whole table."
—Shakespeare, from *Macbeth*

Long life to you.

May your wealth be like the capital of Ireland:
Always Dublin!

To all the days here and after:
May they be filled with fond memories, happiness, and laughter.

May you always have a cool head and a warm heart.

A cheerful glass, a pretty lass,
A friend sincere and true;
Blooming health, good store of wealth
Attend on me and you.

Here's to you:
May you always have a sweetheart, a bottle, and a friend.
The first beautiful, the second full, the last ever faithful.

Here's to prosperity...
and the wisdom to use it well.

I wish thee health,
I wish thee wealth,
I wish thee gold in store,
I wish thee heaven upon the earth.
What could I wish thee more?

While we live,
Let us live.

Here's to good health,
And good thirst to suit!

May you live as long as you like,
And have all you like as long as you live.

May the blessings of each day
Be the blessings you need most.

May the saddest day of your future be no worse
Than the happiest day of your past.

Life is like a cup of tea,
It's all in how you make it!

May you live long,
Die happy,
And rate a mansion in heaven.

Here's to you and yours
And to mine and ours.
And if mine and ours
Ever come across to you and yours,
I hope you and yours will do
As much for mine and ours
As mine and ours have done
For you and yours!

Some friends wish you happiness,
and others with you wealth,
But I wish you the best of all—
contentment blessed with health!

May we have in our arms those we love in our hearts.

Here's to those who love us, and here's to those who don't:
A smile for those who are willing too, and a tear for those who
won't.

To the whole wide world, just in case someone thinks we've forgot.

May your joys be as deep as the oceans,
your troubles as light as its foam,
and may you find, sweet peace of mind,
where ever you may roam.

May you have the hindsight to know where you've been,
the foresight to know where you're going,
and the insight to know when you're going too far.

May you have warm words on a cold evening,
a full moon on a dark night, and a smooth road all the way to
your door.

I wish you health, love, and money, and the time to enjoy them!

May your home always be too small to hold all your friends.

May your glass be ever full.

May you ever have a kindly greeting from them you meet along
the road.

May those who live truly be always believed,
And those who deceive us be always deceived.

Leave the hurry
To the masses;
Now's the time
To drain your glasses.

May you always come more than you go.

Here's health to your enemies' enemies!

May you always dance as if no one were watching,
Sing as if no one were listening,
And live every day as if it were your last.

May you be poor in misfortune,
rich in blessings,
slow to make enemies,
quick to make friends.

But rich or poor, quick or slow,
may you know nothing but happiness
from this day forward.

May there always be work for your hands to do.
May your purse always hold a coin or two.
May the sun always shine warm on your windowpane.
May a rainbow be certain to follow each rain.
May the hand of a friend always be near you.
And may God fill your heart with gladness to cheer you.

Here's my wish for you:
May your glass be ever full.
May the roof over your head be always strong.
And may you be in heaven half an hour before the devil knows
you're dead.

As you slide down the banister of life,
May the splinters never point the wrong way.

Always remember to forget
The things that made you sad.
But never forget to remember
The things that made you glad.

May the blessings of light be upon you,
Light without and light within.
And in all your comings and goings,
May you ever have a kindly greeting
From them you meet along the road.

May brooks and trees and singing hills
Join in the chorus, too.
And every gentle wind that blows
Send happiness to you.

May the face of every good news
And the back of every bad news
Be toward us.

May you have food and raiment,
A soft pillow for your head,
May you be forty years in heaven
Before the devil knows you're dead.

Your health one and all,
from one wall to the other.
And you outside there—
speak up, brother!

Here's to beefsteak when you're hungry,
Whiskey when you're dry,
All the bedmates you'll ever want,
And heaven when you die.

Here's that we may always have
A clean shirt,
A clean conscience,
And a buck in our pocket.

May you live to be a hundred years,
With one extra year to repent!

May I see you bald
And combing your grandchildren's hair.

May the Lord keep you in his hand
And never close his fist too tight.

May your neighbors respect you,
Trouble neglect you,
The angels protect you,
And heaven accept you.

For the test of the heart is trouble
And it always comes with years.
And the smile that is worth the praises of earth
Is the smile that shines through the tears.

May you always have...
Walls for the winds,
A roof for the rain,

Tea besides the fire,
Laughter to cheer you,
And all your heart might desire.

May the joys of today
Be those of tomorrow.
The goblets of life
Hold no dregs of sorrow.

May your heart be warm and happy
With the lilt of Irish laughter
Every day in every way
And forever and ever after.

Wherever you go and whatever you do,
May the luck of the Irish be there with you.

May Dame Fortune ever smile on you, but never her daughter,
Miss Fortune.

May the best of happiness, honor, and fortunes keep with you.

Here's to a full belly, a heavy purse, and a light heart.

May you be merry and lack nothing.

May the rocks in your field turn to gold.

I give you play days, heydays and pay days!

Here's to blue skies and green lights.

May your luck ever spread,
Like jelly on bread.

Here's to good luck 'till we are tired of it.

May the tide of fortune float us into the harbor of content.

May bad fortune follow you all your days and never catch up
with you.

May we all have the unspeakable good fortune to win a true
heart, and the merit to keep it.

May you be as lucky as a mosquito in a nudist colony.

"A flock of blessings light upon thy back."
—William Shakespeare, *Romeo and Juliet*

Two ins and one out:
In health, in wealth, and out of debt.

May the sunshine of comfort dispel the clouds of despair.

May the saints protect you, and sorrow neglect you, and bad luck to the one that doesn't respect you.

May your well never run dry.

May your fire be as warm as the weather is cold.

May we never do worse.

May the clouds in your life be only a background for a lovely sunset.

May the most you wish for be the least you get.

Here's to turkey when you're hungry,
Champagne when you're dry,
A pretty woman when you need her,
And heaven when you die.

In the words of *Star Trek*'s Mr. Spock, "Live long and prosper."

Shakespeare wrote, "Heaven give thee many, many merry days," and I wish the same for all of you.

'Tis hard to tell which is best,
Music, Food, Drink, or Rest.

To my fellow carousers:
As Bertold Brecht once said, "Pleasure seeking is among the greatest virtues. Wherever it is neglected or maligned, something is rotten."

May you always distinguish between the weeds and the flowers.

To the good life:
 To quote Johann Heinrich Voss, he
"Who loves not women, wine, and song,
Remains a fool his whole life long."

Here's to sunshine and good humor all over the world.

May you live to learn well, and learn to live well.

Love to one, friendship to a few, and goodwill to all.

To good will, which Marshall Field called, "the one and only asset that competition cannot undersell or destroy."

Here's to the heart that never wanders and the tongue that never slanders.

May good nature and good sense always be united.

May your pleasures be free from the stings of remorse.

In the words of Bill & Ted, "Party on, dudes" and "Be excellent to each other."

Eat thy bread with joy, and drink thy wine with a merry heart.
Ecclesiastes 9:7

Drink and be merry, for our time on earth is short, and death lasts forever.

A Toast to the Reader

Here's our good wish to you: May you have the opportunity to use every one of these toasts, and make up some of your own, too!

Chapter 6

Humorous Toasts

$\mathscr{T}$oasts are a perfect opportunity to show a little wit. While you're standing up and holding the attention of the room, you might as well make people smile. As in any speaking situation, be aware of your audience. Many well-loved toasts are a little too colorful for more conservative audiences. As with all toasts, keep it short. Audiences no longer have long enough attention spans for the long, "shaggy-dog" stories that my grandfather once used as toasts at the annual meeting of the Wianno Club.

The toasts here, of course, not the only humorous toasts in this book. In almost every section you will find a few toasts that, if delivered with a smile, will amuse your friends.

May you be as happy in life as me and eh... what's her name?

Here's to the married woman:
A mistress of arts, who robs a man of his bachelor's degree and forces him by lectures to study philosophy.

'Tis better to have loved and lost,
Than to marry and be bossed.

Here's to Eve, the mother of all races,
Who wore a fig leaf in all the right places.
Here's to Adam, the father of us all,

Who was "Johnny on the Spot"
when the leaves began to fall.

Here's to the women that I've loved and all the ones I've kissed.
As for regrets, I just have one; that's all the ones I've missed.

Oh, womens' faults are many, us men have only two:
Every single thing we say, and everything we do.

Here's to the maiden of twenty
who knows it's folly to yearn,
And picks a lover of fifty
because he has money to burn.

Here's to that girl who offers her honor:
For all night long I'll be off her and on her.

Let's drink to California, way out by the sea,
Where a woman's ass, and a whiskey glass,
Made a horse's ass of me.

No matter how beautiful,
how smart, or how cute she is...
somebody...somewhere, is sick of her shit!

Here's to the lady who dresses in black,
who always looks sweet and never looks slack.
And when she kisses she kisses so sweet,
she makes things stand that have no feet.

You guys came by to have some fun.
You'll come and stay all night, I fear.
But I know how to make you run.
I'll serve you all the cheapest beer.

Here's to woman, whose heart and whose soul
Are the light and the life of each path we pursue:
Whether sunned at the tropics or chilled at the pole,
If woman be there, there's happiness too.

I love the girls that say they won't.
I love the girls that say they do,
And then they say they don't.

But the girls that I do love the most,
And I know you'll think I'm right,
Are the girls that say they normally don't,
But for you I think I might.

I love them, all the ladies,
With their frilly little things.
I love them with their diamonds,
Their perfumes and their rings.
I love them, all the ladies,
I love them big and small,
But when a lady isn't quite a lady,
That's when I love them most of all.

Here's to woman, who in our hours of ease
Is uncertain, coy, and impossible to please.

Here's to the beautiful woman: The hell of the soul, the purgatory of the wallet, and the paradise of the eyes.

To women:
A paradox who puzzles when she pleases and pleases when she puzzles.

To quote Minna Thomas Antrim, Here's to women who are "clever enough to convince us that we are cleverer than they at their cleverest."

A woman's tongue is only three inches long, but it can kill a man six feet tall.

Here's to woman, the source of all our bliss;
There's a special taste of heaven in her kiss;
But from the queen upon her throne, to the maid in the dairy,
They are all alike in one respect:
They are all quite contrary.

Here's to women:
They're the loveliest flowers that bloom under heaven.

Woman—the morning star of infancy, the day star of manhood, the evening star of old age; bless our stars and may they always be kept at a telescopic distance.

To the bachelor:
A man who prefers to ball without the chain.

Here's to the man who loves his wife,
And loves his wife alone:
For many a man loves another man's wife
When he might be loving his own.

Here's to love: The disease which begins with a fever and ends
with a pain.

To the land we love, and the love we land.

Here's to lovers everywhere—the have-been's, the are-now's, and
the may-be's.

God grant me
the anxiety to try to control the things I cannot control,
the fear to avoid the things I can,
and the neurosis to deny the difference.

Here's to me and here's to you,
And here's to love and laughter.
I'll be true as long as you
But not a single second after!

Here's to the girl I love the best:
I've loved her naked and I've loved her dressed.
I've loved her standing and I've loved her lying.
And if she had wings, I'd love her flying.
And when she's dead and long forgotten,
I'll dig her up and love her rotten.

The only difference between and Irish wedding
and an Irish wake, is one less drunk.

Kings and Queens do it and sigh;
Little bees do it and die.
But I won't do it and I'll tell you why.
I promised my sweetheart I would be true.
So let me tell you what I'll do:
I'll lie still and let you!

Here's to love: A little sighing, a little crying,
a little dying...and a touch of white lying.

A toast to any gentleman
So shrewd and diplomatic
Who never, though he's in his cups,
Decides he's operatic.

Show me the man who has enjoyed his school days and I will
show you a bully and a bore.
—Robert Morley

You can't expect a boy to be vicious
until he's been to a good school.
—Saki (H. H. Munro)

Here's to Hell:
May the stay there
Be as much fun as the way there.

It's easy to be pleasant when life flows by like a song.
But the man worth while is the one who can smile
When everything goes dead wrong.

Here's to fine wine, women, and song.
And here's to workdays that aren't too long.
Here's to shoes that always fit.
And here's to you, you silly shit!

Here's to health and prosperity,
To you and all your posterity.
And them that doesn't drink with sincerity,
That they may be damned for all eternity!

Good day, good health, good cheer, good night!

'Tween wine and women, a man's lot is to smart;
For wine makes his headache, and women, his heart.

Grant me a sense of humor, Lord,
The saving grace to see a joke,
To win some happiness from life,
And pass it on to other folk.

To my Friend:
When you are sad, I will get you drunk and help you plot
revenge against the sorry bastard who made you sad.
When you are blue, I'll try to dislodge whatever is choking you.
When you smile, I'll know you finally got laid.
When you are scared, I will rag you about it every chance I get.
When you are worried, I will tell you horrible stories about how
much worse it could be and tell you to quit whining.
When you are confused, I will use little words to explain it to
your dumb ass.
When you are sick, stay away from me until you're well again. I
don't want whatever you have.
When you fall, I will point and laugh at your clumsy ass.
This is my oath, I pledge 'til the end.
Why you may ask? Because you're my friend!

Accept that some days you're the pigeon
And some days you're the statue.

To eternity:
May it last forever!

Here's to the women who love me terribly,
May they soon improve.

Though life is now pleasant and sweet to the sense
We'll be dead and moldy a hundred years hence.

I drink to your charm, your beauty, and your brains...
which gives you a rough idea of how hard up I am for a drink.
—Groucho Marx

Friends may come, friends may go,
Friends may peter out, you know.
But we'll be friends through thick and thin,
Peter out or peter in.

Don't make love by the garden gate.
Love is blind—but the neighbors ain't!

May the people who dance on your grave get cramps in their legs.
—Yiddish toast

Drinkers of the world unite, you have nothing to lose but your money, your woman, your liver, your kids, your sanity, your job....

Here's to heat:
Not the kind that ignites and burns down shanties
but the kind that exictes...and slides down panties!

May you die in bed at 95 years,
Shot by a jealous spouse!

Twas the month after Christmas, and Santa had flit;
Came there tidings in the mail, which read: Please remit.

Sixty years ago I knew everything. Now, I know nothing.
Education is a progressive discovery of our own ignorance.
—Will Durant

May you:
Work like you don't need the money,
Love like you've never been hurt,
Dance like no one is watching,
Screw like it's being filmed,
And drink like a true Irishman.

May the winds of fortune sail you,
May you sail a gentle sea.
May it always be the other guy
who says, "This drink's on me."

Here's to the game called "Ten Toes"
That's played all over town.
The lassies play with ten toes up.
And the lads with ten toes down!

To women and horses...
And the men that ride them!

May all your ups and downs
come only in the bedroom.

Here's to living single and drinking double.

Here's to bein' single,
drinkin' doubles,
and seein' triple!

Here's to all of the women who have used me and abused
me...and may they continue to do so!

May your liquor be cold,
May your women be hot.
And may your troubles slide off of you
Slicker than snot.

Here's to wives and girlfriends.
May they never meet!

Here's to life—ain't it grand.
Just got divorced from my old man.
I laughed and laughed at the court's decision.
They gave him the kids and they ain't even his'n!

A Toast to the Reader

If you spent your money
On stuff that's funny,
Here's a good bit of it,
Hope you're a hit with it!

Chapter 7

Flirting Toasts

Toasting has long been the perfect way to show a little romantic interest in someone who appeals to you. For a perfect example, think of Humphrey Bogart toasting Ingrid Bergman with "Here's looking at you, kid" in the movie Casablanca. The response you get to your toast can often reveal how the object of your affection feels about you, and, perhaps, how much competition you have. And as the evening wears on, you can use ever more forward toasts.

Not only is it okay to declare your passion in toasts, some people have gotten into trouble for not doing so. The story told in the English folk song "Barbara Allen" is one in which William gets into trouble because he drinks a toast to the ladies in the tavern without first saluting his beloved Barbara Allen. (For the record, we think these folks overreacted a bit. Dying because of a toast is going a bit too far.)

If I had a flower for every time I thought of you,
I could walk through my garden forever.

Here's looking at you
Here's to me and here's to you,
And if in the world
There was just us two
And I could promise that nobody knew
Would you?

Here's to this water,
Wishing it were wine,
Here's to you, my darling,
Wishing you were mine.

Here's to you, I love you.
I love you because you're good
You're good because God made you.
And Goddamn I wish I could.

Here's to your eyes, Here's to my eyes.
Here's to your thighs, Here's to my thighs.
Our eyes have met, our thighs not yet...
But here's hoping.

To women:
The crown of creation.

To women and wine:
Both are sweet poison.

To wine and women:
May we always have a taste for both.

Here's to women, the ultimate aristocrats:
They govern without law and decide without appeal.

Women:
The fairest work of creation; the edition being extensive, let no
man be without a copy.

Here's to the ladies:
First in our hearts and first in our wallets.

Here's to woman:
The fair magician who can turn man into an ass and make him
think he's a lion.

May we kiss all the women we please, and please all the women
we kiss.

Here's to our sweethearts and our wives;
May our sweethearts soon become our wives,
And our wives ever remain our sweethearts.

Here's to the gladness when she's glad,
Here's to the sadness of her sadness when she's sad;
But the gladness of her gladness,
And the sadness of her sadness,
Are nothing compared to the madness of her madness
when she's mad.

A toast of wine, to woman divine,
I would drink in haste, me think;
To her eyes, to her hair, to her beauty so rare—
But I haven't the wine to drink.

Here's to the ladies:
You can't live with them and you can't live without them.

Here's to Woman:
A mistress of arts, who robs a man of his bachelor's degree and
forces him by lectures to study philosophy.

The ladies, God bless them,
May nothing distress them.

Here's to the prettiest, here's to the wittiest,
Here's to the truest of all who are true,
Here's to the nearest one, here's to the sweetest one,
Here's to them, all in one—here's to you.

Here's to the woman that's good and sweet,
Here's to the woman that's true,
Here's to the woman that rules my heart—
In other words, Here's to you.

To the Ladies:
We admire them for their beauty, respect them for their
intelligence, adore them for their virtue, and love them because
we can't help it.

In the immortal words of Ambrose Bierce,
"Here's to woman—ah, that we could fall into her arms without
falling into her hands."

To woman:
The only loved autocrat who governs without law and decides
without appeal.

Here's to the light that lies in women's eyes,
And lies, and lies and lies.

May our women distrust men in general, but not us in particular.

Here's to God's first thought, Man!

Here's to God's second thought, Woman!
Second thoughts are always best,
So here's to Woman!

"What, sir, would the people of earth be without woman? They would
be scarce, sir, almighty scarce."
—Mark Twain

To the lovely ladies. May they always heed the wise words of
Ralph Waldo Emerson who said that "The only gift is a portion of
thyself."

"And nature swears, the lovely dears
Her noblest work she classes, O;
Her 'prentice hand she tried on man,
And then she made the lasses, O."
—Robert Burns

To women, whose beauty and wisdom are proof of the existence of
a higher power.

Here's to the girls of the American shore,
I love but one, I love no more;
Since she's not here to drink her part,
I drink her share with all my heart.

Here's to women—the fairest work of the Great Author. The edition
is large and no man should be without a copy.

Here's to the girl with eyes of blue,
Whose heart is kind and love is true;
Here's to the girl with eyes of brown,
Whose spirit proud you cannot down;
Here's to the girl with eyes of gray,
Whose sunny smile drives care away:
Whate'er the hue of their eyes may be,
I drink to the girls, this toast with thee!

Here's to a girl who's bound to win
Her share at least of blisses,
Who knows enough not to go in
When it is raining kisses.

Here's to the game called "Ten Toes"
That's played all over town.
The lassies play with ten toes up.
And the lads with ten toes down!

Here's to all of the women who have used me and abused me...
And may they continue to do so!

A book of verses underneath the bough,
A jug of wine, a loaf of bread, and thou.
—Omar Khayyam

To the life we love with those we love.

"Drink to me only with thine eyes,
And I will pledge with mine;
Or leave a kiss within the cup,
And I'll not look for wine."
    —Ben Jonson

Here's to the girl I love; and,
Here's to the girl who loves me.
Here's to those who love the girl I love,
And, all those who love the girl I love who love me.

I drink to the health of another,
And the other I drink to is he
In the hope that he drinks to another,
And the other he drinks to is me.

Wine, to strengthen friendship and light the flame of love.

To Cupid, whom George Farquhar called, the "blind gunner."

Here's to love, a thing so divine,
Description makes it but the less.
'Tis what we feel, but cannot define,
'Tis what we know but cannot express.

"A mighty pain to love it is,
And 'tis a pain that pain to miss;
But, of all pains, the greatest pain,
Is to love, but love in vain."
—Abraham Cowley

Wine comes in at the mouth
And love comes in at the eye;
That's all that we will know for truth
Before we grow old and die.
I lift the glass to my mouth,
I look at you and I sigh.
—William Butler Yeats

To quote John Keats's immortal line,
"A thing of beauty is a joy forever."
Here's to these beautiful bridesmaids.

Here's to women:
They're the loveliest flowers that bloom under heaven.

"I have a dozen healths to drink to these fair ladies."
—Shakespeare, from Henry VIII

Here's to those'd love us
If only we cared.
Here's to those we'd love
If only we dared.

A Toast to the Reader

Here's to the people
That authors need
People buying books
And who like to read.

Chapter 8

Patriotic Toasting

*T*oasting has always been a way of showing loyalty. In more formal times, there was a strict order in which toasts were to be made, and the first toast was always to the king, queen, president, etc. While you are less likely today to be thrown out of a gathering for starting with something other than a toast of allegiance, it is still appropriate to use toasting as an opportunity to show your stripes (and stars).

To the American eagle:
May it never rise in anger, never go to roost in fear.

May the pinions of the American eagle spread the pinions of liberty throughout the world.

To freedom from mobs as well as kings.

Love, life and liberty.
Love pure,
Life long,
Liberty boundless.

Our hearts where they rocked our cradle.
Our love where we spent our toil,

And our faith, and our hope and our honor,
We pledge to our native soil.
—Rudyard Kipling

To the United States. We may have our critics, but, as the saying
goes, "Immigration is the sincerest form of flattery."

May we always remember what red, white and blue really stand
for—love, purity and fidelity.

Here's a health to America, the pride of the earth,
The stars and the stripes—drink the land of our birth!
Toast the army and navy who fought for our cause,
Who conquered and won us our freedom and laws.

May every patriot love his country, whether he was born in it or
not.

Here's to America, or in the words of Oliver Wendell Holmes,
"One flag, one land, one heart, one hand, one nation evermore."

Here's to America. In the words of Stephen Decatur,
"...our country right or wrong."

To America. As Carl Schurz once said, "Our country! When
right, to be kept right. When wrong, to be put right!"

To the land we love, and the love we land.

May the seeds of dissention never find growth in the soil of
America.

To the land we live in, love and would die for.

Here's to the Army and Navy,
And the battles they have won,
Here's to America's colors—
The colors that never run.

The union of lakes, the union of lands,
The union of states none can sever,
The union of hearts, the union of hands,
And the flag of our union forever.

To the United States, where each man is protected by the Constitution regardless of whether he has ever taken the time to read it.

In the words of David Starr Jordan, "Rome endured as long as there were Romans. Americans will endure as long as we remain American in spirit and thought."

To America, may we always be, as Omar Bradley said, "an arsenal of hope."

Here's to America and England. In the words of Charles Dickens, "May they never have any division but the Atlantic between them."

Here's to America and England. To quote George Bernard Shaw, here's to "two countries separated by the same language."

To America, may we never lose sight of the fact that we are, in the words of Adlai Stevenson, "the first community in which men set out to institutionalize freedom, responsible government, and human equality."

Here's to the American eagle—the liberty bird that permits no unjust liberties.

We've toasted all names and all places,
We've toasted all kinds of game,
Why not just for loyalty's sake
Drink one to our nation's name.

"To her we drink, for her we pray,
Our voices silent never;
For her we'll fight, come what may,
The stars and stripes forever."
—Stephen Decatur

The Lily of France may fade,
The Thistle and Shamrock wither,
The Oak of England may decay,
But the Stars shine on forever.

America! My country, great and free.
Heart of the world, I drink to thee.

To America. Let us always remember that the last two syllables of American are, "I CAN."

"Millions for defense, but not one cent for tribute."
—Robert Goodloe Harper, at a banquet for John Marshall, June 18, 1798

A Toast to the Reader

Here's to the country
That you like the most.
Now you can say so
In a patriotic toast.

Chapter 9

International Toasting

People toast all over the world. Different cultures have different rituals. When in a foreign culture, it is best to ask your host or guide, before an event, what sort of toasting is likely to go on. Unless someone tells you that you are expected to make the first toast, it is best to let others start things off and to follow what other guests do.

Different Toasts for Different Folks

To give you an idea of how much toasting can vary, here's how my sister Victoria describes the festivities that celebrated her marriage to someone from the Bahnar ethnic group, one of the Vietnamese tribal groups generally referred to as Montagnards or hill tribes.

"The wedding reception was held outdoors, in the afternoon, if I remember correctly. People would come and set up their wine jars in the courtyard of the house. These are big jars about two and a half to three feet high. The drink itself is made by preparing a fermented mash of rice or corn at the bottom of the jar. When it is time to celebrate, water is poured over the mash and two straws are stuck in.

"Over the course of the afternoon as the level of the rice wine goes down, people add more water. Consequently, those who drink from a jar early on often get a very strongly alcoholic drink. Those who drink later get a more watered down version.

"As the newlyweds, we would go to visit each family at their jar. The head of family would wish us a long and happy marriage, give us their gift, and we would drink from their jar. My husband generally replied to their comments, and I just smiled, since I didn't have any great fluency in the language."

In contrast, a business associate provided the following guidelines for traditional Japanese toasting. She also noted that younger people often toast in a, more-or-less, American style.

"We do not stand. Since we sit on the floor, it would get a bit tiring to stand up and sit back down repeatedly.

"We do not drink until the word "Kanpai" is said, usually by the head of the group. "Kanpai" literally means "dry cup."

"As in other Asian countries, we empty our cups when we toast, especially at the first toast. Since Japanese cups are relatively small, we can have many toasts.

"The most popular "Kanpai" drinks are beer and sake."

Don't be alarmed if a foreign toast sounds nonsensical, or even a bit aggressive. We were bemused when we first heard the French say "Merde" as they tossed back wine that was certainly not merde-like. But we later came to realize that this toast is no less, and no more, sensible than our familiar "Here's mud in your eye."

Cautionary Tales

Ask more than one person, when you can, to make sure that you have solid information about foreign toasting customs. Here are a few anecdotes that emphasize why you should do this:

When our friends Rob and Ellen got married, I thought it would be both clever and appropriate to give a toast in Norwegian to salute her family. We asked a Norwegian business associate for an appropriate comment. He supplied a toast to the effect of "Skal de ha flere ar, og mange, mange barne mor." I knew enough Norwegian to know that it meant, "May you live long and have many children." What I didn't

know was that when I uttered those words I would be pronouncing a
song title that half the room then expected me to lead them in singing.

At least that was a benevolent mistake. One of my business associates
was told, before his first trip to Japan, that he would offend his hosts if he did
not come to the first dinner, after he landed, wearing only the small robe that
hung on the back of his hotel room door. This seemed quite challenging
since he was well over six feet tall, so he arrived first and practiced sitting
modestly on the floor. His hosts, who showed up in impeccable Brooks Brothers
suits, were not impressed. The guy who gave him the false information laughed
for weeks.

A friend of mine thought she was being savvy when she proposed a
toast "To the Queen" in a friendly bar in the United Kingdom. To her
surprise, she discovered that the traditional response to that toast in
the particular pub in a corner of Ireland that she was in is "Fuck the
Queen!"

The final, and absolutely necessary cautionary tale has to do with
driving customs as well as drinking customs. A friend, who has been in
the United States for many years, grew up in Europe and never forgot
the toasting customs. What he did forget after a night of toasting, was
that they drive on the other side of the road in some countries. The
steering wheel placement should have been a reminder. Luckily, he
met a police officer and not an untimely end.

Some Handy Foreign Toasts

While you rarely want to start the toasting, I have always found
that people appreciate it if you try and participate in a toast in their
language. Ask someone to say the word for you, as the spellings and
pronunciations vary. For example, one person explained that the way
to pronounce the Irish toast "Slainté" is to slur the sentence "It's a lawn
chair."

Albanian: Gezuar.
Arabian: Bismillah, Fi schettak.
Armenian: Genatzt.
Austrian: Prosit.
Belgian: Op uw gezonheid.
Brazilian: Saude. Viva. Felicidades.
    Una pro santo!

Chinese: Nien Nien nu e. Kong Chien.
    Kan bei. Yum sen. Wen ule.
Czechoslovakian: Na Zdravi. Nazdar.
Danish: Skal.
Dutch: Proost. Geluk.
Egyptian: Fee sihetak.
Esperanto: Je zia sano.
Estonian: Tervist.
Finnish: Kippis. Maljanne.
French: A votre santé, Bon Santé, Santé, Merde.
German: Prosit. Auf ihr wohl.
Greek: Eis Igian.
Greenlandic: Kasugta.
Hawaiian: Okole maluna. Hauoul maoul oe. Meul kaulkama.
Hebrew: L'chaim.
Hungarian: Kedves egeszsegere.
Icelandic: Santanka nu.
India: Apki Lambi Umar Ke Liye.
Irish: "Céad Míle Fáilte, Sláinte.
Italian: A la salute. Salute. Cin cin.
Japanese: Kampai. Banzai.
Korean: Kong gang ul wi ha yo.
Lithuanian: I sveikas.
Malayan: Slamat minum.
Mexican: Salud.
Moroccan: Saha wa'afiab.
New Zealander: Kia ora.
Norwegian: Skal.
Pakistani: Sanda bashi.
Philippine: Mabuhay.
Polish: Na zdrowie. Vivat.
Portuguese: A sua saude.
Romanian: Noroc. Pentru sanatatea dunneavoastra.
Russian: Na zdorovia.
Spanish: Salud. Salud, amor y pesetas y el tiempo para gustarlos!
    Salud, pesetas y un par de tetas.
Swedish: Skal.
Thai: Sawasdi.
Turkish: Serefe.

Ukrainian: Boovatje zdorovi.
Welsh: Iechyd da.
Yugoslavian: Zivio.

The World Cup of Toasting

These phrases are just the beginning. In many areas, the tradition of longer, more elaborate toasting lives on. If there were an international toasting competition, several countries would be sure to make the finals. Russia and many of the former Soviet Republics would be strong contenders. Sweden, from my experience, would be in the fray. And the descendants of Shakespeare in England would have to be reckoned with. However, there's a good chance that the championship would be decided between the Irish and the Scottish.

Irish Toasting

I have never experienced Irish toasting in County Mayo, but I have witnessed this gentle folk art in various parts of what some call County New York and County Boston. It is, mostly, gentle. No one wishes friends well more wistfully and more sincerely than the Irish. Just as many Americans have Irish ancestors, many of the toasts in this book started in Ireland. Here are a few samples:

May your neighbors respect you,
Trouble neglect you,
The angels protect you,
And heaven accept you.

May the Irish hills caress you.
May her lakes and rivers bless you.
May the luck of the Irish enfold you.
May the blessings of Saint Patrick behold you.

May your thoughts be as glad as the shamrocks.
May your hearts be as light as a song.
May each day bring you bright happy hours,
That stay with you all year long.

For each petal on the shamrock
This brings a wish your way.
Good health, good luck, and happiness
For today and every day.

May your heart be warm and happy
With the lilt of Irish laughter
Every day in every way.
And forever and ever after.

Wherever you go and whatever you do,
May the luck of the Irish be there with you.

May your blessings outnumber
The shamrocks that grow,
And may trouble avoid you
Wherever you go.

Here's to the land of the shamrock so green,
Here's to each lad and his darling colleen,
Here's to the ones we love dearest and most,
And may God Bless old Ireland!—that's an Irishman's toast.

If you're enough lucky to be Irish...
You're lucky enough.

Marry a mountain girl
and you marry the whole mountain.

Health and a long life to you.
Land without rent to you.
A child every year to you.
And if you can't go to heaven,
May you at least die in Ireland.

May the luck of the Irish possess you.
May the devil fly off with your worries.
May God bless you forever and ever.

May you have:
No frost on your spuds,
No worms on your cabbage.
May your goat give plenty of milk.

And if you inherit a donkey,
May she be in foal.

To Ireland, the place on earth
That heaven has kissed
With melody, mirth,
And meadow and mist.

Scottish Toasting

The Scots are, most days of the year, less loquacious than the Irish. On the birthday of the poet Robert Burns (and, incidentally, this author's birthday), they hold an annual party at which both the toasting and the food are formidable.

If you are interested in the toasting tradition, befriend a few Scots and get yourself invited to a "Burns Supper." They are steeped in lore and tradition, as well as good Scotch. The toasts are made in the accented dialog in which Burns wrote. For some reason, they make more sense and are easier to follow as the feast goes on.

The "Selkirk Grace," which precedes the meal, is familiar to many:
Some hae meat, and canna eat,
And some wad eat that want it;
But we hae meat, and we can eat
And sae the Lord be thankit.

One of the popular toasts is Here's Tae Us:
Here's tae us
Wha's like us
Damn few,
And they're a' deid
Mair's the pity!

You'll hear these two poems at virtually every Burns Supper. At the more elaborate ones, you will also be treated to recitals of long passages and perhaps a bit of bagpiping.

A Toast to the Reader

While people around the world toast differently, almost everyone likes to toast. Let's drink to that common ground!

Chapter 10

Diplomatic Toasts

oasting has always been the perfect way for diplomats and heads of state to salute each other. If you become interested in this kind of toasting, you'll find details of toasts in the reports from almost every summit. There is a good deal of information about official toasts in various countries available online. The Web site for Alberta, Canada, for example, is quite prescriptive:

"A toast to The Queen should be proposed at all official functions attended by the Lieutenant-Governor (LG) when a meal is served. It should take place at the end of the meal, or at the end of the meal course, not at the beginning of the meal. The LG is always happy to propose the toast.

"The wording should be "The Queen of Canada" or "The Queen" and no remarks should be added. A good formula is for the host or chairman to rise and ask the LG to propose the toast to The Queen of Canada. Everyone is thus forewarned and the LG can simply raise his/her glass and make the toast.

"If a band is in attendance at a formal dinner and it is wished to have a musical salute and a toast, the LG should stand and propose the toast, at which time the band plays a full verse of "God Save The Queen." Those assembled toast The Queen after the band stops playing.

"If the host or chairman wishes to toast the Governor General, should he/she be present, or the Lieutenant-Governor and his/her spouse, he should not do so immediately after the toast to The Queen.

"Note: No smoking should be allowed until after the Toast to The Queen has been proposed."

That's just the rules for one situation. There are different rules for when this toast, The Loyal Toast, is executed at a military meal.

US Diplomatic Toasting

Occasionally, you can read about amusing mistakes, such as the time President Reagan toasted the people of Bolivia when he should have said Brazil. These, however, are rare exceptions. For the most part, US officials have toasted well, following a precedent set by Ben Franklin, whose wit made him the toast of Paris.

The story goes that Franklin found himself at a party with a Frenchman and an Englishman. The Englishman proposed a toast to "Great Britain, the sun that gives light to all nations of the earth." The Frenchman answered with a toast to "France, the moon whose magic rays move the tides of the world." Franklin rose to the situation with a toast to "our beloved George Washington, the Joshua of America, who commanded the sun and the moon to stand still—and they obeyed."

Years later, at a more formal occasion in 1961, President John F. Kennedy made a more diplomatic toast in which he managed to compliment the French while also claiming a special place for the United States.

"As an American I take pleasure in seeing people around the world salute the American Revolution and the principles for which we fought. As Frenchmen, I know that you take satisfaction that people around the world invoke your great motto of Liberty, Equality and Fraternity. What counts, of course, is not merely the words, but the meaning behind them. We believe in liberty and equality and fraternity. We believe in life and liberty and the pursuit of happiness. And we believe that the rights of the individual are preeminent, not merely the slogans and the mottoes which are invoked across the globe by those who make themselves our adversary. We believe in the significance behind these great ideas. Therefore, I think it quite natural that in the most difficult decade of the 1960's, France and the United States should be once again associated together.

"It is a particular source of satisfaction to me as President of the United States that we should be associated with President DeGaulle. He stands now as the only great leader of World War II who occupies a position of high responsibility. The others have gone and he remains, and he stands true to the same concept which he fought for during the Second World War, the sovereignty of France, the community of the Western Nations. And therefore, as a junior figure on this field, which he has occupied for more than twenty years, I ask you to drink to the great Captain of the West, your President, General DeGaulle."

A Toast to the Reader

While Presidents, Kings, Queens, and Ministers change, the tradition of diplomatic toasting clearly endures. Here's hoping all future conflicts are solved over glasses, and not on the battlefield.

Chapter 11

Toasts about Drinking

Much toasting is about drinking. People like to toast the very idea of drinking, and often they like to toast their favorite drinks.

Man, being reasonable, must get drunk;
The best of life is but intoxication.
—Lord Byron

Here is a toast to lying, cheating, drinking, and stealing:
If you lie, lie only to keep a friend.
If you cheat, may you cheat death.
If you steal, steal your lover's heart.
If you drink, drink deeply of the joy of your new life together.

Work is the curse of the drinking class.
—Oscar Wilde

We are all of us in the gutter.
But some of us are looking at the stars.
—Oscar Wilde

It is better to spend money like there's no tomorrow
then to spend tonight like there's no money.
—P.J. O'Rourke

The problem with some people is that
when they aren't drunk they're sober.
—William Butler Yeats

"Then here's to the heartening wassail,
Wherever good fellows are found;
Be its master instead of its vassal, and order the glasses around."
—Ogden Nash

Here's to cheating, stealing, fighting, and drinking.
If you cheat, may you cheat death.
If you steal, may you steal a woman's heart.
If you fight, may you fight for a brother.
And if you drink, may you drink with me.

Here's to swearing, lying, stealing, and drinking.
When you swear, swear by your country;
When you lie, lie for a friend;
When you steal, steal away from bad company;
And when you drink, drink with me.

Lift 'em high and drain 'em dry
To the guy who says, "My turn to buy!"

In all this world, why I do think
There are four reasons why we drink:
Good friends,
Good wine,
Lest we be dry,
And any other reason why!

Clink, clink your glasses and drink;
Why should we trouble borrow?
Care not for sorrow,
A fig for the morrow.
Tonight let's be merry and drink.

Here's to Miguel de Cervantes who said, and I quote, "I drink when I have occasion and sometimes when I have no occasion."

A glass in the hand is worth two on the shelf.

To drinking: Better to pay the tavernkeeper than the druggist.

"Here's lookin' at you, kid!" —Rick in *Casablanca.*

To drinking together, the safest form of sex ever invented.

Down the hatch!

Here's mud in your eye!

Cheers!

Cheers, cheers, now bring more beers.

May we always mingle in the friendly bowl,
The feast of reason and the flow of the soul.

"What harm in drinking can there be?
Since punch and life so well agree?"
—Thomas Blacklock

Come fill the bowl, each jolly soul!
Let Bacchus guide this session;
Join cup to lip with 'hip, hip, hip'
And bury all depression.

To quote from an old drinking song,
"Come, landlord, fill the flowing bowl
Until it does run over
For tonight we'll merry be, merry be, merry be,
Tomorrow we'll get sober."

"The man that isn't jolly after drinking
Is just a driveling idiot, to my thinking."
—Euripides

Bottoms up,
Tops down;
Wear a smile
Not a frown.

May we never want a friend to cheer us, or a bottle to cheer him.

Up to my lips and over my gums; look out guts, here she comes.

Here's a health to the king and a lasting peace.
To faction an end, to wealth increase;
Come, let's drink it while we have breath,
For there's no drinking after death.
And he that will this health deny
Down among the dead men let him lie!

Here's to a sweetheart, a bottle, and a friend.
The first beautiful, the second full, the last ever faithful.

When we drink, we get drunk.
When we get drunk, we fall asleep.
When we fall asleep, we commit no sin.
When we commit no sin, we go to heaven.
So, let's all get drunk, and go to heaven!

May the beam of the glass never destroy the ray of the mind.

"For, whether we're right or whether we're wrong,
There's a rose in every thistle
Here's luck—
And a drop to wet your whistle."
—Richard Hovey

One glass is wholesome, two glasses toothsome, three glasses blithesome, four glasses fulsome, five glasses noisome, six glasses quarrelsome, seven glasses darksome.

As Tom Waits says, "I'd rather have a free bottle in front of me, than a pre-frontal lobotomy!"

"Fill the goblet again! For I never before
Felt the glow which now gladdens my heart its core;
Let us drink!
Who would not?
Since through life's varied round
In the goblet alone no deception is found."
—Lord Byron

Here's to your welcome which was cordial, and your cordial which is welcome.

I love to drink martinis.
Two at the very most.
Three I'm under the table.
Four I'm under the host!
—Dorothy Parker

Here's to the great artistic genius, Pablo Picasso;
His last words were "Drink to me." Who am I to question genius?

On land or at sea
One need not be wary:
A well-made martini
Prevents beri beri.

Best while you have it use your breath
There is no drinking after death.

Drink is the feast of reason and the flow of soul.
—Alexander Pope

No animal ever invented anything as bad as drunkenness,
Or as good as drink.

I have taken more out of alcohol than alcohol has taken out of
me.
—Winston Churchill

To friends—as long as we are able
To lift our glasses from the table.

"But fill me with the old familiar juice,
Methinks I might recover bye and bye."
—Omar Khayyam

In the immortal words of William Makepeace Thackeray,
"I drink it as the Fates ordain it,
Come, fill it, and have done with rhymes;
Fill up the lonely glass, and drain it
In memory of dear old times."

Merry met, and merry part,
I drink to thee with all my heart.

In the words of William Morris, "I drink to the days that are."

Here's the drinker's last request:
"When I die, don't bury me at all,
Just pickle my bones in alcohol:
A scuttle of booze
At my head and shoes,
And then my bones will surely keep."

The Frenchman loves his native wine;
The German loves his beer;
The Englishman loves his 'alf and 'alf,
Because it brings good cheer.
The Irishman loves his whisky straight,
Because it gives him dizziness.
The American has no choice at all,
So he drinks the whole damned business.

There are many good reasons for drinking
And one has just entered my head—
If a man can't drink while he's living
How the hell can he drink when he's dead!

Here's to the dove that flies above
and never sheds a feather.
If I can't be with the one I love
I'll be drinkin' this stuff forever.

Here's to those who wish us well,
as for the rest, they can go to Hell!

Moderation is a fatal thing—nothing succeeds like excess.
—Oscar Wilde

A glass in the hand's worth two on the shelf—
Tipple it down and refresh yourself!

Here's to you,
And here's to me.
Friends forever we will be.
And if we should ever disagree,
Then fuck you, too, here's to me.

Here's to the women upon the shore;
I love but one, I love not more.
But since she's not here to drink her part,
I'll drink her share with all my heart.

Here's to the perfect girl,
I couldn't ask for more.
She's deaf 'n dumb, oversexed,
and owns a liquor store.

Here's to living single and drinking double!

Here's to bein' single...
drinkin' doubles...
and seein' triple!

The horse and mule live thirty years
And never knows of wines and beers.
The goat and sheep at twenty die
Without a taste of scotch or rye.
The cow drinks water by the ton
And at eighteen is mostly done.
The dog at fifteen cashes in
Without the aid of rum or gin.
The modest, sober, bone-dry hen
Lays eggs for noggs and dies at ten.
But sinful, ginful, rum-soaked men
Survive three-score years and ten.
And some of us...though mighty few
Stay pickled 'til we're ninety-two.

A true drinker is never drunk as long as
He can hold onto one blade of grass and not
fall off the face of the earth.

May you:
Work like you don't need the money,
Love like you've never been hurt,
Dance like no one is watching,
Screw like it's being filmed,
And drink like a true Irishman.

He's a fool who give over the liquor,
It softens the skinflint at once,
It urges the slow coach on quicker,
Gives spirit and brains to the dunce.
The man who is dumb as a rule
Discovers a great deal to say,
While he who is bashful since Yule
Will talk in an amorous way.

It's drink that uplifts the poltroon
To give battle in France and in Spain,
Now here is an end of my turn—
And fill me that bumper again!

Then to our final toast tonight,
our glasses freely drain,
Happy to meet, sorry to part,
happy to meet again.

Beer and Ale

Be one who drinks the finest of ales.
Every day without fail.
Even when you have drank enough,
Remember that ale is wonderful stuff.

Give a man a fish and he will eat for a day.
Teach him how to fish and he will sit in a boat
and drink beer all day.

In heaven there is no beer...
That's why we drink ours here.

Here's to a long life and a merry one.
A quick death and an easy one.
A pretty girl and an honest one.
A cold beer—and another one!

He that buys land buys many stones.
He that buys flesh buys many bones.
He that buys eggs buys many shells,
But he that buys good beer buys nothing else.

For every wound, a balm.
For every sorrow, cheer.
For every storm, a calm.
For every thirst, a beer.

On the chest of a barmaid near Yale
Were tattooed the prices of ale.
And on her behind,
For the sake of the blind,
Was the same information in Braille!

Fill with mingled cream and amber,
I will drain that glass again.
Such hilarious visions clamber
Through the chambers of my brain.
Quaintest thoughts—queerest fancies,
Come to life and fade away:
What care I how time advances?
I am drinking ale today.
—Edgar Allan Poe

In Vino Veritas
In Cervesio Felicitas
(Roughly, "In wine there is wisdom, In beer there is joy.")

Here's a toast to the roast that good fellowship lends,
With the sparkle of beer and wine;
May its sentiment always be deeper, my friends,
Than the foam at the top of the stein.

I won't drink beer with any man
That won't drink beer with a Harvard fan.

The best beer is where priests go to drink.
For a quart of Ale is a dish for a King.
—Shakespeare, "A Winter's Tale"

Here's to what we drink. History flows forward on rivers of beer.

Here's to beer, and its role in our history. After all, the
Ship's log of the Mayflower read, "For we could not
now take time for further search (to land our ship) our
victuals being much spent, especially our Beere."

But the greatest love—the love above all loves,
Even greater than that of a mother...

Is the tender, passionate, undying love,
Of one beer drunken slob for another.
—Irish ballad

Payday came and with it beer.
—Rudyard Kipling

You foam within our glasses, you lusty golden brew,
Whoever imbibes takes fire from you.
The young and the old sing your praises,
Here's to beer,
Here's to cheer,
Here's to beer!
—From the opera, *The Bartered Bride*
by Bedrich Smetana, 1866

Life, alas,
Is very drear.
Up with the glass,
Down with the beer!
—Louis Untermeyer

May your Guardian Angel always be at your side to
pick you up off the floor and hand you another cold
one from the store.

Dough, the stuff that buys me beer.
Ray, the guy who brings me beer.
Me, the guy who drinks the beer.
Far, a long way to get beer.
So, I'll have another beer.
La, I'll have another beer.
Tea, no thanks I'm having beer.
That will bring us back to...
...DOH!!!
—Homer Simpson

You guys came by to have some fun.
You'll come and stay all night, I fear.
But I know how to make you run.
I'll serve you all the cheapest beer.

A statesman is an easy man, he tells his lies by rote.
A journalist invents his lies, and rams them down your throat.
So stay at home and drink your beer and let the neighbors vote.
—William Butler Yeats

I like beer. On occasion, I will even drink beer to
celebrate a major event such as the fall of communism
or the fact that the refrigerator is still working.
—Dave Barry

Without question, the greatest invention in the history of
mankind is beer.
Oh, I grant you that the wheel was also a fine invention,
but the wheel does not go nearly as well with pizza.
—Dave Barry

"I have a total irreverence for anything connected with society,
except that which makes the road safer, the beer stronger,
the old men and women warmer in the winter, and happier in the
summer."
—Brendan Behan

Let no man thirst for lack of Real Ale.
—Motto of the *Commonwealth Brewing Co.*, Boston

Champagne costs too much,
Whiskey's too rough,
Vodka puts big mouths in gear.
This little refrain
Should help to explain
Why it's better to order a beer!

Some Guinness was spilt on the barroom floor
When the pub was shut for the night.
When out of his hole crept a wee brown mouse
And stood in the pale moonlight.
He lapped up the frothy foam from the floor
Then back on his haunches he sat.
And all night long, you could hear the mouse roar,
"Bring on the goddamn cat!"

When money's tight and hard to get
and your horse is also ran,
When all you have is a heap of debt
a pint of plain is your only man.

If at church they'd but give some ale
And a pleasant fire for our souls to regale
We'd sing and we'd pray all the livelong day
Nor ever once from the church to stray.

Beer drinkin' don't do half the harm of love makin'.
—Old New England proverb

Nary a day goes by that I miss to wonder why
the moon shows his face as the day draws nigh.
In the firelight I ponder my canine's thought
as he gazes upon me from his hand-me-down cot.
I think of God and all his creations,
one being the women with her unbridled temptations.
I have searched for love with no direction,
skeletons in the closet... a fine collection.
These quandries of mine, I'm sure to figure out.
For I know the answer lies at the bottom of this stout.

Of all my favorite things to do,
the utmost is to have a brew.
My love grows for my foamy friend,
with each thirst-quenching elbow bend.
Beer's so frothy, smooth and cold—
It's paradise—pure liquid gold.
Yes, beer means many things to me...
Right now it means I gotta pee!

Why, if 'tis dancing you would be,
There's brisker pipes than poetry.
Say, for what were hop yards meant,
Or why was Burton built on Trent?
Oh many a peer of England brews
Livelier liquor than the Muse,
And malt does more than Milton can
To justify God's ways to man.
Ale, man, ale's the stuff to drink.

For fellows whom it hurts to think:
Look into the pewter pot
To see the world as the world's not.
—A.E. Housman

In the words of the old ballad,
"He that drinketh strong beer and goes to bed right mellow,
Lives as he ought to live and dies a hearty fellow."

O thrice accursed
Be a champagne thirst
When the price of beer's all we've got.

Let's drink the liquid of amber so bright;
Let's drink the liquid with foam snowy white;
Let's drink the liquid that brings all good cheer;
Oh, where is the drink like old-fashioned beer?

W. L. Hassoldt said it best,
"None so deaf as those who will not hear.
None so blind as those who will not see.
But I'll wager none so deaf nor blind that he
Sees not nor hears me say come drink this beer."

Who'd care to be a bee and sip
Sweet honey from the flower's lip
When he might be a fly and steer
Head first into a can of beer?

Such power hath beer.
The heart where
Grief hath cankered
Hath one unfailing remedy—the tankard.

'Twas ever thus from childhood's hour,
I've seen my fond hopes disappear;
I've always had a champagne thirst,
But have to be content with beer.
Beer makes you feel the way you ought to feel without beer.
—Henry Lawson

A mouth of a perfectly happy man is filled with beer.
—Egyptian Wisdom, c. 2200 B.C.

Champagne

Here's to the members of the Cliquot Masters club. (You know who you are.)

Here's champagne to your real friends
And real pain to your sham friends!

The miser may be pleased with gold,
The lady's man with pretty lass;
But I'm best pleased when I behold
The nectar sparkling in the glass.

To champagne—a beverage that makes you
see double and feel single.

Here's to champagne, a drink divine
That makes us forget our troubles;
It's made of a dollar's worth of wine,
And twenty bucks worth of bubbles

To champagne—
Nectar strained to finest gold,
Sweet as Love, as Virtue cold

"Some take their gold
In minted mold,
And some in harps hereafter,

"But give me mine
In bubbles fine
And keep the change in laughter."
—Oliver Herford

May we always be as bubbly as this champagne.

Coffee

To strong, hot coffee
It's what I'll take
Tomorrow morning
For my headache.

To Coffee—
Black as the devil,
Strong as death,
Sweet as love, and
Hot as hell!

To a hot, steaming cup of Joe
Tomorrow when I wake up slow.

To Coffee—
Life would truly be obscene
Without occasional caffeine.

Rum

Drink rum, drink rum,
Drink rum, by gum with me,
I don't give a damn
For any damn man
That won't take a drink with me.

Seeing this motley crew gathered here this evening, I'm reminded
of a toast made famous by Robert Louis Stevenson.
"Fifteen men on the Dead man's Chest—
Yo-ho-ho and a bottle of rum!
Drink and the devil had done for the rest—
Yo-ho-ho and a bottle of rum!"

"Don't die of love; in heaven above
Or hell, they'll not endure you;
Why look so glum when Doctor Rum
Is waiting for to cure you?"
—Oliver Herford

Whiskey

A toast to the three great American birds:
May you always have an eagle in you pocket,
A chicken on your table,
And Wild Turkey in your glass.

Four blessings upon you...
Older whiskey
Younger women
Faster horses
More money.

Let's drink to California, way out by the sea,
Where a woman's ass, and a whiskey glass,
Made a horse's ass of me.

Here's to women's kisses,
and to whiskey, amber clear;
not as sweet as a woman's kiss,
but a damn sight more sincere!

In the words of Oliver Goldsmith,
"Let schoolmasters puzzle their brains
With grammar and nonsense and learning;
Good liquor I stoutly maintain,
Gives genius a better discerning."

Here's to whisky, scotch, or rye,
Amber, smooth, and clear;
It's not as sweet as a woman's lips,
But a damn sight more sincere.

Here's to the best key for unlocking friendship—whiskey.

Keep your head cool and your feet warm,
And a glass of good whiskey will do you no harm.

In the immortal words of Ogden Nash, "Candy is dandy, but
liquor is quicker."

May your liquor be cold,
May your women be hot.
And may your troubles slide off of you
slicker than snot.

Here's to Ms. C. O. Smith who said it best when describing the
ideal way to drink one's liquor,
"How beautiful the water is!
To me 'Tis wondrous sweet—
For bathing purposes and such;
But liquor's better neat."

May we never be out of spirits.

Wine

When wine enlivens the heart
  May friendship surround the table.

Give me wine to wash me clean
From the weather-stains of care.
  —Ralph Waldo Emerson

In water one sees one's own face;
But in wine one beholds the heart of another.
—French proverb

Here's to the wine we love to drink, and the food we like to eat.
Here's to our wives and sweethearts, let's pray they never meet.

"To the corkscrew—a useful key to unlock the storehouse of wit,
the treasury of laughter, and front door of fellowship, and the gate
of pleasant folly."
—W. E. P. French

Any port in a storm. Or any wine, for that matter.

To grape expectations.

Let us acknowledge the evils of alcohol and strive to eliminate
the wine cellar—one glass at a time.

To wine, it improves with age:
The older I get, the more I like it.

God, in His goodness, sent the grapes
To cheer both great and small;
Little fools will drink too much,
And great fools none at all.

A feast is made for laughter, and wine maketh merry.
Ecclesiastes 10:19

Drink no longer water, but use a little wine for thy stomach's
sake. I *Timothy* 5:23

Give...wine unto those that be of heavy hearts
Proverbs 31:6

Wine maketh glad the hearts of man.
Psalms 104:15

Wine nourishes, refreshes and cheers. Wine is the foremost of
medicines...wherever wine is lacking, medicines become
necessary.
—The Talmud

Wine, which cheereth God and man.
Judges 9:15

I'm partial to the logic of James Howell who once said,
"Good wine makes good blood;
Good blood causeth good humors;
Good humors cause good thoughts;
Good thoughts bring forth good works;
Good works carry a man to heaven.
Ergo: Good wine carrieth a man to heaven."

To quote George Sterling,
"He who clinks his cup with mine,
Adds a glory to the wine."

Wine and women:
May we always have a taste for both.

Wine, to strengthen friendship and light the flame of love.

To women and wine:
Both are sweet poison.

"'Tis a pity," said Lord Byron, "wine should be so deleterious,
For tea and coffee leave us much more serious."

Here's to wine, wit, and wisdom.
Wine enough to sharpen wit,
Wit enough to give zest to wine,
Wisdom enough to "shut down" at the right time.

The best wine...that goeth down sweetly, causing the lips of those
that are asleep to speak.
Song of Solomon 7:9

Wine was created from the beginning to make men joyful, and
not to make men drunk. Wine drunk with moderation is the joy
of the soul and the heart.
Ecclesiastes 31:35-36

In the words of Jonathan Swift, "This wine should be eaten, it is
too good to be drunk.

To wine—those plump grapes' immortal juice
That does this happiness produce.

"This bottle's the sun of our table.
Its beams are rosy wine;
We, planets that are not able
Without its help to shine."
—R. B. Sheridan

To wine:
May those who use it never abuse it.

"Then fill the cup, fill high! fill high!
Nor spare the rosy wine,
If death be in the cup, we'll die—
Such death would be divine."
—James Russell Lowell

Here's to the red and sparkling wine,
I'll be your sweetheart, if you'll be mine,
I'll be constant, I'll be true,
I'll leave my happy home for you.

Fill up boys, and drink a bout;
Wine will banish sorrow!
Come, drain the goblet out;
We'll have more tomorrow!

Give me a bowl of wine—in this I bury all unkindness."
Shakespeare, *Julius Caesar*

Drink to me only with thine eyes,
And I will pledge with mine;
For I would have to pawn my watch
If she should drink more wine.

"God made Man,
Frail as a Bubble
God made Love
Love made Trouble
God made the Vine
Was it a Sin
That Man made Wine
To drown Trouble in?"
—Oliver Herford

Here's to mine and here's to thine!
Now's the time to clink it!
Here's a bottle of fine old wine,
And we're all here to drink it.

Here's to old wine and young women.

A Toast to the Reader

May all your drinks
be flavored with toasts.

Afterword
Toast Responsibly

oasting is a wonderful thing to do. Please don't give it a bad name.

If you think people are getting too drunk to understand what you are saying, stop toasting.

If you want to slow down your consumption at an event where there's lots of toasting, try a trick I learned after a dinner in which everyone was toasting with sake. Start holding your glass high so people can't see that you're just taking sips, rather than draining the glass. This works best if you are tall and if you are toasting with containers that aren't transparent, such as sake cups.

∞

A Toast to the Reader

Here to happy toasting for us all!

Index

About the Author

A ndrew Frothingham, a member of the Author Guild, holds two Harvard degrees and has held many glasses aloft toasting. In addition to helping executives in many industries find the right words for all kinds of occasions and media, he has written and cowritten books for toasters and speakers including: *Last Minute Speeches and Toasts, Creative Excuses, And I Quote, Well-done Roasts,* and *Crisps Toasts.* He and his wife and two sons live in the Tribeca section of Manhattan.